To my hunt-loving
husband : Doug
With love -
Jill
1996

Elk

Behavior • Ecology • Conservation

Text by Erwin A. Bauer
Photography by Erwin and Peggy Bauer

Voyageur Press

Dedication

This book is dedicated to all who have worked to save the North American wilderness. Especially important are the great continuing conservation efforts of the Foundation for North American Big Game, Greater Yellowstone Coalition, Boone and Crockett Club, Canadian Nature Federation, Defenders of Wildlife, Montana Wilderness Association, National Audubon Society, National Wildlife Federation, National Parks and Conservation Association, Nature Conservancy, Pope and Young Club, Rocky Mountain Elk Foundation, Seirra Club, Whitetails Forever, Wilderness Society, Wildlife Conservation Society, and the World Wildlife Fund.

Edited by Michael Dregni
Designed by Andrea Rud
Printed in China

96   97   98   99   5   4   3   2   1

Library of Congress Cataloging-in-Publication Data

Bauer, Erwin A.
Elk : behavior, ecology, conservation / text by Erwin A. Bauer ; photography by Erwin and Peggy Bauer.
        p.   cm.
Includes bibliographical references (p. 157) and index.
ISBN 0-89658-275-2
1. Elk—North America.   I. Bauer, Peggy.   II. Title.
QL737.U55B376   1996
599.73'57—dc20   95-24582
                                        CIP

Distributed in Canada by Raincoast Books, 8680 Cambie Street, Vancouver, B.C. V6P 6M9

Published by Voyageur Press, Inc.
123 North Second Street, P.O. Box 338, Stillwater, MN 55082 U.S.A.
612-430-2210, fax 612-430-2211

Please write or call, or stop by, for our free catalog of natural history publications. Our toll-free number to place an order or to obtain a free catalog is 800-888-WOLF (800-888-9653).

Educators, fundraisers, premium and gift buyers, publicists, and marketing managers: Looking for creative products and new sales ideas? Voyageur Press books are available at special discounts when purchased in quantities, and special editions can be created to your specifications. For details contact the marketing department.

Page one: Bull elk of similar size spar in a tournament that begins before the rut and continues until the dominance—strength—of one over the other is determined. Page three: Antlers polished and throat swollen, a large bull elk bugles across an open autumn meadow.

Contents

Introduction

First Encounters with Elk

Although it seems (and almost is) a lifetime ago, I will always remember the happy golden summer of 1935. A young man just graduated from high school, I vagabonded westward from Ohio and found a job in Yellowstone National Park. It was menial work at low pay: swabbing boats and dressing trout for tourists at the outlet of Yellowstone Lake. But no matter, because I also discovered an invigorating new world. In my spare time I was free to explore the first and the finest of all our national parks. That experience set the course for the rest of my life. Too suddenly that summer idyll ended when the time came to return home to my first semester at college.

Before we left, a friend and I decided to make one final, farewell, overnight hike into the lonely Yellowstone back country. Nightfall found us rolled up in blankets under the stars near a trail that paralleled Hellroaring Creek. We fell asleep immediately, despite the hard ground; we had no tent or true sleeping bags back then.

Sometime during the night I heard an eerie, unsettling sound that was somewhere between a squeal and a giant flute or calliope echoing from the black night. At first it seemed to be a bad dream, but it grew louder and more shrill, coming nearer and nearer when I sat up shivering. An answer always came from somewhere farther in the distance. It wasn't until the cold and frosty dawn that we finally saw the bugler. A huge antlered beast, its breath white and its dark body steaming, was prancing and tearing up turf on an open grassy slope just above us. That strange spectacle in the dim, blue light was more than enough to stop my shivering. It was also my introduction to the North American elk, second largest of all the world's deer, and the species that many outdoors people consider the greatest of all big-game animals.

Following an early autumn storm, a bull elk emerges from the Absaroka-Beartooth Wilderness Area in Montana.

Since that time I have had more than my share of experiences with elk throughout its range, eventually living in the best elk country of Wyoming and Montana. This region happens to include some of the deepest, most beautiful wilderness left in our land.

One especially vivid encounter occurred on Christmas Eve during the first year after Peggy and I arrived in Jackson Hole in 1971. A savage winter storm was dumping a heavy snow on the Snake River Valley late that afternoon as Peggy and I drove northward from shopping in the town of Jackson toward our home on the edge of Grand Teton National Park. We learned from the car radio that most highways in the area had already been closed and that soon the road we were driving on would also be impassable. We were meeting no other traffic on the road and visibility was almost zero. As we approached a bridge that spans the Gros Ventre River, I had to hit the brakes suddenly to avoid striking a bull elk that appeared directly in our path. We skidded to a stop and found ourselves in the midst of a herd of bulls. Altogether we counted at least twenty-five antler racks above the swirling snow, all crossing in front of us and plunging through deep drifts toward the National Elk Refuge nearby, where they would safely spend the winter. What a remarkable Christmas gift it was to see them. Never before or since that day have I seen so many bulls together.

Several other memorable meetings with elk also come to mind. I think of the cow elk fleeing the terrible Yellowstone forest fires of 1988, but pausing long enough in midstream of the Gardiner River to nurse her calf. I also think of another cow that managed to outrun a grizzly bear while probably saving a small calf that was hiding where it had been born not long before.

There is also that morning on my last hunt for elk a quarter century ago before exchanging my gun for

Left: Early on a foggy morning, a bull bugles from its bed in a frosty meadow. Other elk nearby are obscured by the fog. Overleaf: A view of Jackson Hole, Wyoming, the valley of the Snake River, from near Deadman's Bar, in golden autumn when elk move into this valley from summer range in the surrounding mountains.

camera and telephoto lenses. Outfitter Gap Puchi and I were up well before dawn, saddling horses and riding out of his base camp high in Wyoming's Teton Wilderness. It was bitterly cold, especially for early September, as we urged the horses up a steep, rough trail in total darkness toward an area where alpine meadows divided dark, timbered islands. At first glow of light in the east, we tied up the horses and continued on foot to where we overlooked a long, narrow meadow surrounded by trees. We crouched behind a deadfall, to wait there until the morning light was brighter. Then, blowing into a length of plastic tubing, Gap imitated exactly the bugling I had heard that morning long ago when boyhood ended in Yellowstone Park. Almost immediately he had an answer. From deep inside the dense green spruce just opposite us a bull called back. Gap waited a few minutes and bugled again. Next thing I knew a fine male elk, with ivory tips on its brown antlers, was prancing and digging at the frosty ground in full view, exactly like the elk bull near Hellroaring Creek. But unlike that first one, this bull was suspicious. Some sixth sense seemed to warn that it had been duped. Almost as magically as it had appeared, it was gone. Not even Gap Puchi's virtuoso efforts could coax it back out into the meadow. But from far back in the timber, the bull kept answering Gap's challenge . . . just in case.

The pursuit of elk, as well as the other wild creatures that share its range, has taken Peggy and me to many of North America's most beautiful and precious wild places. It has also made us more determined to help save as much of this land as possible intact and undisturbed, for the future. In this way we will also save the elk.

At sunset a bull elk continues its search for cows to fill its breeding harem. The search may cover great distances.

North American Elk:
Monarchs of the Forest

Whoever considers themselves beautiful after seeing me has no heart.
—**Song of the elk, according to the Sioux Elk Society, from Thomas E. Mails,**
Dog Soldiers, Bear Men and Buffalo Women

As recently as 120,000 years ago, there were no elk in North America. About that time great glaciers expanded from polar regions into temperate parts of the earth, freezing enough water so that the level of the world's oceans dropped more than three hundred feet (90 meters). This drop in sea level exposed a land bridge between Siberia and Alaska that remained in place until the end of the Ice Age. At the same time, elk, or red deer, living in Tibet or western China's Tien Shan Mountains began to expand their range in all directions. Animals moving westward became the numerous subspecies of red deer that inhabit much of Eurasia today, ranging as far west as Scotland and as far south as Iran and India. Those that walked eastward made their way over the land bridge to Alaska and then gradually ranged southward. By the time Christopher Columbus reached the West Indies in 1492, elk were the most widespread of all hoofed animals in the New World. In the journals of the historic Meriwether Lewis and William Clark expedition across America in 1804–1806, there are 570 references to the elk the explorers found almost everywhere. That is no longer true today as the elk range has decreased over the last two centuries, while the whitetail deer range has greatly expanded.

An elk of the Rocky Mountain subspecies (Cervus canadensis nelsoni) *crosses a creek to drive away a rival bull that is approaching too near to its harem. If the rival does not retreat, a fight will ensue.*

How the name of this handsome animal originated remains unclear and is often debated. The name *elk* may have come from an ancient Greek word for "stag," or from the Latin *alces*, which also translates as "stag." More likely it derives from the German *elg* or *elch*, or the Norse *elgr*, or old English *alke*, again translating as "deer" or "stag." But no matter really. By the 1800s elk was the accepted name almost everywhere in the new United States and Canada.

Since then a few writers, especially Europeans, have called elk *wapiti*, and we still see that name of Native American origin used occasionally to lend a romantic touch. But *wapiti*, which is a Shawnee word for "white rump," never really caught on. To almost all biologists and outdoorspeople today, the elk is an elk.

Evolution of the Elk

Strange as it may seem, taxonomists do not agree on how to classify the North American, or New World, elk. Some still call it *Cervus canadensis*, a separate and distinct species, and one of the forty species of deer surviving on earth today. Others are convinced that our elk is *Cervus elaphus*, and therefore exactly the same animal as the red deer that roams across much of Europe and Asia. Elk and red deer can and do interbreed when one is introduced into the range of the other.

There is agreement that there were six subspecies of either *C. canadensis* or *C. elaphus* living in North America when the human migration from Europe began about four hundred years ago. However, it is difficult for anyone except a trained and fully equipped game technician to detect the minor physical differences and to positively tell an individual of one subspecies from another.

Eastern Elk (*Cervus canadensis canadensis*)

The first elk encountered by the first wave of settlers on the Atlantic Coast was *Cervus canadensis canadensis* (or *C. elaphus canadensis*). Florentine explorer Giovanni da Verrazano first described them in New England in 1524. A few years later, Frenchman Jacques Cartier wrote of seeing "great stores of Stages [stags]" during his historic voyage up the Saint Lawrence River. This race of elk once occupied the vast deciduous forests of eastern and southeastern Canada and the United States as far west as a line drawn between Arkansas, Minnesota, and western Ontario, except for a narrow coastal strip along the Atlantic Ocean.

But the Eastern elk was gradually eliminated; it was a large, easy target even for early firearms, and was a victim of the rapid loss of its woodland habitat. In 1851, naturalist and artist John James Audubon noted that only a few were left in the Allegheny Mountains and almost none anywhere else. Today *C. canadensis canadensis* is extinct, and what little we know about this eastern race comes from skulls and a skeleton in the Smithsonian Institution collection and in other museums.

Merriams's or Desert Elk (*Cervus canadensis merriami*)

Nor do we know much about *C.c. merriami*, Merriams's elk, also known as the desert elk. It lived in a few mountain ranges of Arizona, New Mexico, Texas, and the northern Mexican states of Sonora, Chihuahua, and Coahuila. Written records about this race are rare and contradictory, but it may have been the largest of all the elk. A casualty of range overgrazed by domestic livestock, the last of this subspecies disappeared sometime between 1902 and 1906.

Tule or Dwarf Elk (*Cervus canadensis nannodes*)

During the summer of 1579, the English explorer Sir Francis Drake is believed to have been the first European to sight and record elk along the Pacific Coast. Today these elk, *C.c. nannodes*, the Tule or dwarf elk, are endangered as well. Restricted to semidesert southern California, this sub-species required the most specialized habitat of all elk. Herds once roamed in the Sacramento and San Joaquin Valleys, but they could not compete with the introduction of the Spaniard's livestock and rifles, as well as the later demands for meat by the expanding human population, especially in the gold-mining camps.

If not for the concern of one landowner, Henry Miller, three centuries later, the Tule elk would also have been extirpated. Rancher Miller sheltered a few animals on his own property until the Tule Elk Refuge was established in Kern County in 1934. Most of the eight hundred to nine hundred Tule elk living today are on or near this last refuge.

Manitoban or Plains Elk (*Cervus canadensis manitobensis*)

During the halcyon times when bison by the millions

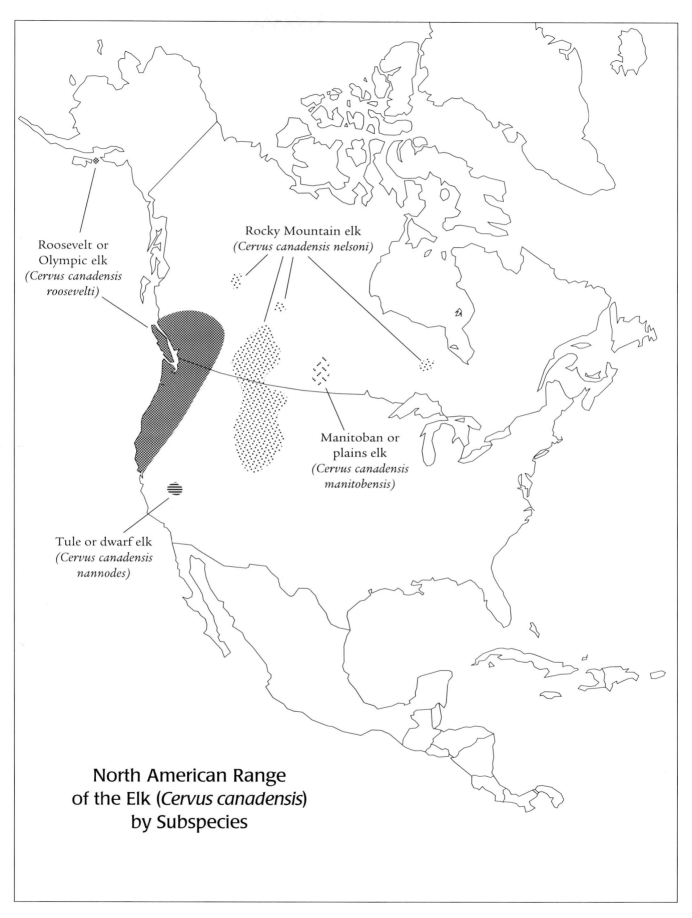

Roosevelt or
Olympic elk
*(Cervus canadensis
roosevelti)*

Rocky Mountain elk
(Cervus canadensis nelsoni)

Manitoban or
plains elk
*(Cervus canadensis
manitobensis)*

Tule or dwarf elk
*(Cervus canadensis
nannodes)*

North American Range
of the Elk (*Cervus canadensis*)
by Subspecies

*Above: The Manitoban or plains elk subspecies (*Cervus canadensis manitobensis) *survives only in national and provincial parks in Manitoba and Saskatchewan.* *Right: A Roosevelt or Olympic elk (*Cervus canadensis roosevelti) *bull emerges from a dark evergreen forest into the early morning sunshine of the Pacific Northwest.*

Almost all of the Tule or dwarf elk subspecies (Cervus canadensis nannodes) left on earth live today on or near the Tule Elk Refuge in southern California. At one time they were almost extirpated by market hunters and a loss of habitat to domestic livestock.

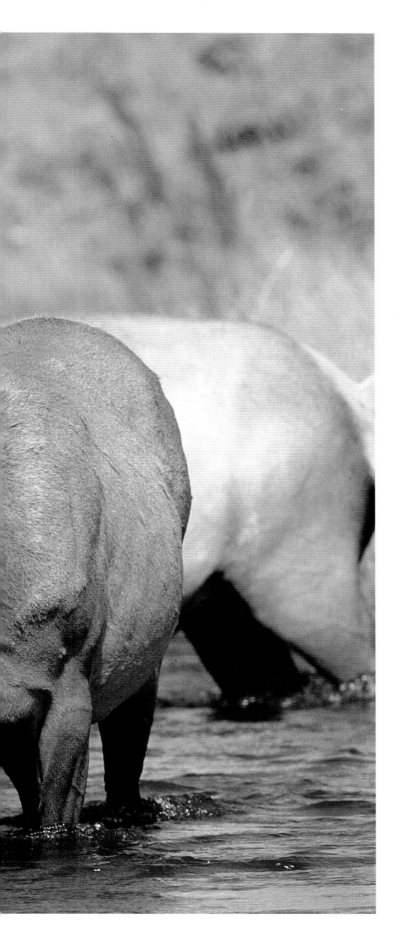

occupied the Great Plains, the second-most-abundant large mammal was the plains or Manitoban elk, *C.c. manitobensis*. But like the buffalo, their numbers diminished during the westward expansion; they were the victims of the same old problems: loss of environment and over-shooting.

Plains elk are slightly darker, and on the average, the males have smaller antlers than other subspecies. About 9,500 exist today, almost all in Canadian sanctuaries: Riding Mountain National Park and Duck Mountain Provincial Park in Manitoba, and Prince Albert National Park in Saskatchewan.

Roosevelt or Olympic Elk (*Cervus canadensis roosevelti*)

Roosevelt or Olympic elk, *C.c. roosevelti*, are natives of the Pacific coastal mountain ranges from northern California redwood country northward to British Columbia, including Vancouver Island. This subspecies has also been introduced and thrives on Afognak Island, Alaska. It is the largest of all today's elk, both in body size and in average antler dimensions. Although meat and hide hunting during the mid-1980s exterminated these elk from the southernmost portion of their range, their population has been holding steady for several decades, thanks to sound management and hunting regulations.

Rocky Mountain Elk (*Cervus canadensis nelsoni*)

By far the most abundant, most widespread, and second-largest race is the Rocky Mountain elk, *C.c. nelsoni*. Originally these occupied all of the Rocky Mountains and adjacent ranges from Utah and northern New Mexico north through Alberta and British Columbia almost all the way to the Yukon and Northwest Territories border. That range is somewhat narrowed today, but their numbers are stable (or even increasing locally) in what is left. Small scattered herds exist from Texas north into the Midwest, but these were animals transplanted (largely) from Yellowstone National Park. The largest elk populations in 1996 are in Colorado, Wyoming, Montana, Idaho, and Alberta.

Rocky Mountain elk cows pause during a Yellowstone stream crossing. Harem "areas" are often bounded by streams or water barriers making it easier for the bull to patrol and defend.

Above: A Roosevelt bull has gathered its harem in a meadow of Olympic National Park, Washington, where the subspecies is native and numerous. *Right:* The Mission Mountains form a backdrop for this fine bull of Montana's National Bison Range, a refuge it shares with pronghorn antelope, deer, and large herds of buffalo.

Despite the loss of two races and the near loss of a third, elk have fared fairly well in North America, especially when compared to some other species such as bighorn sheep, bison, gray wolves, musk ox, woodland caribou, and grizzly bears. When he published his *Lives of Game Animals* in 1927, the pioneer naturalist Ernest Thompson Seton estimated that there were ten million elk roaming the continent prior to the arrival of European colonists. That figure may be high, according to some biologists. Still, by 1907 only about 100,000 of all six subspecies could be accounted for and the population was still in decline. In 1922 the number was approximately 90,000 with more than a third of those elk in northwestern Wyoming and Canada. The number is estimated at about 500,000 as the twentieth century comes to a close.

Physical Characteristics of Elk

In 1637 English naturalist T. Morton wrote of three types of deer he found in New England: moose, elk, and whitetail deer. Of the elk he wrote: "it is swift of foote, but of a more dark coloure [than whitetails]; with some griseld heares, when his coate is full growne in the summer season; his hornes grow curing, with a croked beame, resembling our redd Deare, not with a palm like the fallow Deare." That seemingly quaint description still describes the elk today, but let's examine the species in more detail.

My overall impression of elk is of a powerful, well-proportioned animal that is agile and a tenacious survivor; it is easy to understand the description "monarch of the forest" in relation to elk. I have heard an individual bull make enough noise as it walked through a woods to sound like a dozen elk in a hurry. But I have also seen whole herds pass by as silently as field mice. This might be the wildest and most majestic of all American deer.

Fully adult males, five or more years old, average 700 pounds (300 kg), but might reach 1,000 pounds (450 kg). Females weigh 450–500 pounds (200–225 kg). This weight is carried on skeletons that weigh about 100 pounds (45 kg) for bulls and 90 pounds (40 kg) for cows. Mature bulls measure four and one-half to five feet (135–150 cm) high at the withers and eight to nine and one-half feet (240–285 cm) in overall length. Single calves weigh about 35 pounds (15 kg) at birth. The calves are spotted, with the spots disappearing at about three months of age.

In summer the coats of Rocky Mountain elk are a light reddish brown to medium reddish brown, becoming slightly darker in autumn. Males tend to be lighter in color than females. The bull elk has a distinctive dark mane on the underside of its neck.

All elk replace all of their hair twice each year, in spring and again in fall. The summer coat is lighter in weight and density than the winter coat, which is somewhat darker in color to both absorb and retain heat from the sun. During the two shedding periods, elk have a disheveled or scruffy look and do not appear to be as robust and healthy as they probably are. Elk also may be less active during shedding periods, when hair is scattered widely to be recycled by nature.

The footprint of an elk has the same characteristic shape of all North American even-toed ungulates, or hoofed animals. It is a two-sided pattern slightly tapered toward the front, with rounded tips. Moose tracks, by comparison, are larger and have more-pointed tips; deer tracks are smaller and heart-shaped. When elk walk over soft ground, or when they run, the dew claws might show in the tracks as a single indentation at the back. When running, the halves of each hoof flare apart to provide greater stability and to reduce sinking into the moist ground.

Next to footprints, an elk's passage is most easily noted by its droppings. As with many herbivores, these droppings are in pellet form, sometimes clustered, medium to dark brown in color, and mushy if the vegetation eaten was succulent. In summer elk may defecate as often as twenty times a day, each time leaving behind more than a hundred pellets.

Elk are highly social animals, which is characteristic of ungulates that spend time, or live together, on fairly open landscapes. They are mainly grass eaters. Especially when feeding out in the open, most of a herd will have heads down, probably with eyes below the level of the grass. But at least one or two animals will be on sentry duty with heads up at all times, scanning all around for approaching danger. When grazing, herd animals are most vulnerable to such predators as mountain lions that hunt by stealth.

It is difficult—perhaps impossible—to measure or compare the senses of elk to those of other wild creatures or of man. But anyone who has ever spent much time afield hunting elk knows too well that their senses of smell, sight, and especially of hearing are extremely keen, many times sharper than the hunter's own. More than once we have been busy photographing one animal or a herd only to realize that these individuals knew that other elk—or a grizzly bear—were approaching long before we could see or hear the intruders ourselves. A bull can hear a rival male bugling far away and well beyond the hearing range of humans standing nearby. I am convinced that elk vision is as good, or certainly almost as good, in darkness as it is in sunny daylight.

Even when compared to most other animals, the elk has immense stamina. Badly injured or wounded elk might travel days and great distances to avoid hunters or predators. I have seen whole herds struggle through deep snow drifts without hesitation during late fall and early winter migrations. They are strong swimmers, and nothing, not even ice-choked rivers, will make them detour from regular travel routes.

Elk are also excellent climbers. At times during midsummer, I have met them high in bighorn sheep and mountain goat country, maybe trying to escape the season's biting insects in the trees and meadows below. My friend Gap Puchi once commented, half seriously, that elk simply sought out high places just for the cool breezes and spectacular views. Peggy and I once discovered a herd of cows and calves that had climbed to the top of Obsidian Cliff in Yellowstone Park and bedded down there in the July sunshine. Who knows for what reason?

Like other mammals living in cold or temperate zones, elk have relatively larger brains than animals of similar size living in warmer latitudes. This helps explain their high learning ability and their adaptability. More keenly than other ungulates, they realize the danger of humans and are wary around them. But they also soon learn where they are safe (in refuges) and will be fed (as in today's winter feeding grounds).

The quaking aspens in the distance have just turned to yellow, and this fine bull is still sleek and fat after a summer of heavy feeding, before the furious rutting season begins in Yellowstone National Park.

Track Comparison of Elk With Other Adult North American *Cervidae*

Whitetail deer (Odocoileus virginianus) and Mule deer (Odocoileus hemionus)
Length: Approximately 3 inches (7½ cm)
Distance between tracks: 20 inches (50 cm)

Elk (Cervus canadensis)
Length: Approximately 4½ inches (11¼ cm)
Distance between tracks: 24–36 inches (60–90 cm)

Caribou (Rangifer caribou)
Length: Approximately 4 inches (10 cm) without dew claws
Distance between tracks: 20–40 inches (50–100 cm)

Moose (Alces alces)
Length: Approximately 7 inches (17½ cm)
Distance between tracks: 24–60 inches (60–150 cm)

Diet of the Elk

The elk's diet is vast, and they at least sample most of the plants where they live year around, browsing and grazing. Biologists know that the elk herds of one mountain range depend on certain plants that may not even exist on adjacent mountain ranges. Pioneer elk researcher Olaus Murie tried to determine the food preferences of elk during many years of directly watching the animals forage and by examining both their range and stomach contents. Thus he was able to list hundreds of plant species that were eaten. But in an interview before he died, Murie admitted to me that his list was far from complete.

I have seen elk avidly eating the flowers, stalks, and tender seed pods of bear grass, the spectacular, tall, white-flowering plant that is common in northwestern Montana; mountain sorrel of the buckwheat family, which is known to be rich in vitamin C; and elk thistle, which is a favorite early summer food that

bears also relish. I have also watched elk munch on fireweed, cow parsnip, scarlet falsemallow, American bistort, and penstemmon. Elk readily browse on serviceberry, golden currant, and chokecherry, but instinctively avoid the green leaves of chokecherry, which are toxic. Elk also avoid purple larkspur, which contains poisonous alkaloids in spring, but they feed heavily on it during late summer when the toxicity apparently disappears after the plants bloom. But elk never eat the widespread mountain death camas, which we identify by its dull white flowers. This plant is as deadly to men and their livestock as it is to wildlife.

Elk rarely pass up the twig ends and winter buds of red osier dogwood. In fact they like this slender, palatable, and nutritious shrub with reddish bark so well that it is often overgrazed. Bitterbrush, with its yellow, roselike blooms, which might be abundant from the lowest valleys to about 9,000 feet (2,700

Facing page, top: Once the rut—the annual breeding season—begins, there is little rest for the alert herding bull that must always be on the lookout to keep its harem intact. Facing page, bottom: Areas such as this in the Bow River Valley of Banff National Park, Alberta, are the wintering ranges of large numbers of elk.

Above: *A cow elk travels along Yellowstone's Firehole River in search of the rank grasses exposed at water's edge by the current. Thermal activity keeps the Firehole River from freezing even during the coldest winters.* **Left:** *This cow in Jasper National Park, Alberta, is coming into estrus and the herd bull follows her every step, even into the Athabasca River.*

Above: A cow browses on the ripe red hips of wild rose growing in Yellowstone National Park. *Right:* Elk thistle, growing here in Wyoming's Snake River Valley, is a nutritious food of elk herds that linger here in late summer. It is also a favorite food of mule deer and bears. *Facing page:* Almost everywhere in elk country, calves are born at about the same time of year as the arrowleaf balsamroot flowers come into full bloom. *Overleaf:* This Yellowstone bull is not quite large or powerful enough yet to command a harem of its own. Still, it prowls the fringes of the harem herds, waiting for any chance to move in.

Elk "Ivory": Hunting for Wealth and Prestige

Even after an elk dies and begins to decay, its teeth remain intact and will remain after everything else has crumbled to dust. The teeth are said to last longer than the life of a man, and thus the elk tooth became an emblem of a long life.
—Laura C. Martin, *Wildlife Folklore*

The elk's upper canine teeth were once in high demand in North America as a prestigious type of false "ivory." Around the turn of the century, there was a wide-scale hunt for elk buglers to make into jewelry and for curiosity value, a massive hunt that seems almost unreal today.

Thousands of elk were slaughtered during the 1930s just to retrieve the canines, which were made into watch fobs, tie clasps, and key-ring ornaments for members of the fraternal Benevolent and Protective Order of Elks. In addition, some dental technicians made false teeth for humans from elk ivory, which was considered ideal due to its hardness. Eventually the wanton killing of elk created such a great outcry that state and federal law officials in the West cracked down and finally stopped it.

These same canine teeth were once of great value to Native Americans. The "ivories," which are about the size and shape of a man's thumb, although flatter, were used for trading and as decorations in beads, pendants, and necklaces. Among many tribes these ivory teeth were equivalent to an early gold standard. To own a lot of buglers was to be rich and influential. On display at the Buffalo Bill Historical Center in Cody, Wyoming, is a beautiful Native American buckskin dress completely covered with hundreds of elk canines. Both the owner and wearer must have been extremely wealthy, considering the length of time that would be required to bargain for or to kill so many elk.

A beautiful Kiowa dress from about 1900 made of deer hide and decorated with seeds, glass beads, and hundreds of elk "ivory" teeth. Both the owner and wearer of this dress must have been extremely wealthy, considering the length of time that would be required to bargain for or to kill so many elk. (Courtesy Buffalo Bill Historical Center, Cody, WY/Gift of William D. Owsley)

meters), is also often overgrazed when the season is dry, when other plants do not mature, and when times in general are hard. Elk may even turn to yellow-flowered cinquefoil, which grows on thin soils from Colorado north to Alaska and has low forage value. But the cinquefoil withstands heavy use by elk, and range managers often examine this plant for evidence of overgrazing or of general elk range health. Many different kinds of clover grow in elk country everywhere, and most are readily consumed. Many western ranchers might also (ruefully) add hay, baled or stacked for their livestock, to any list of important elk foods. It is true that during severe winters standard barbed wire fences are never barrier enough to keep herds away from alfalfa hay. In addition, many elk are sustained over winter by browsing willow.

Whatever the food, elk eat as much as quickly as they can; their four-chambered stomachs make this possible. The first chamber, called the rumen, is really only a holding tank. Elk gulp down vegetation until the rumen is full and then bed down some-where to digest this food. They may retreat to a forest where they are inconspicuous, or they may bed right where they have been browsing. I have even seen elk lying on the remaining patches of melting snow on hot days when insects were swarming.

Wherever it rests, the elk regurgitates food (called cud) from the rumen into the mouth. Now the cud is more thoroughly chewed and this time swallowed into a second stomach called the reticulum where it is further digested. From here the food passes along into the third (omasum) and fourth (abomasum) chambers. From the abomasum the nutrition is finally extracted and absorbed into the animal's body to be used for energy and growth. The remainder is eliminated as dark brown pellets or clusters of pellets. Areas heavily used or preferred by elk are always marked by an abundance of elk droppings.

Both male and female elk are equipped with well-developed upper canine teeth, also called buglers, bugle teeth, whistlers, or tusks. Unlike the canines of carnivores, which are pointed, those of elk are rounded, extremely hard, and ivory-like.

Elk Country

This scenery already rich pleasing and beautiful was still further hightened by immense herds of
Buffaloe, deer Elk and Antelopes which we saw in every direction feeding on the hills and plains.
—Meriwether Lewis, *The Journals of Lewis and Clark,*
September 17, 1804, in the Dakotas

One morning toward the end of July, I hiked up steep mountain trails into a meadow high in Wyoming's Tetons that was ideal elk summer range. Because the day was hot and sunny, when I found a camping spot, I slipped free of the backpack straps and sat down to enjoy a candy bar before pitching my small, lightweight tent. I guess I dozed, because the next thing I knew, I was startled by two Clark's jays, or nutcrackers, fighting over my candy, which had rolled some distance away as I drifted off to sleep.

Before night fell on that idyllic place, I saw still other creatures within sight of my lonely camp: mountain chickadees, white-crowned sparrows, a golden eagle, a yearling mule deer buck, a pika, several yellow-bellied marmots and Uinta ground squirrels, as well as fresh tracks and droppings of elk. Unfortunately there were also mosquitoes. Here was ample evidence that Rocky Mountain elk share their range, no matter what the time of year, with more wild creatures and plants than I could ever list. In fact all of these share—and are interdependent parts—in the same ecosystem.

While munching a cold cereal breakfast the next morning, I spotted two shy cow elk with calves; they could not have picked a more exquisite place to spend the summer. The open mountain slopes all around were a carpet—almost a catalog—of the local wildflowers in season: scarlet Indian paintbrush and penstemmon, larkspur and lupine, all in various shades of blue and at the height of their bloom. I recall a moment of sadness that morning when I realized that too many wild places such as this one are too quickly disappearing in North America and the world.

A bull elk finds only enough forage to survive, under the crusted snow near Beryl Springs in Yellowstone National Park.
Winter is a time of severe test for the species.

The World of the Elk

Elk country anywhere in North America is scenic—sometimes spectacularly scenic—the kind of wilderness that offers escape and renewal for anyone who relishes the outdoors. From summer through fall it is made to order for hiking, exploring, and for wildlife watching with a day pack or a rucksack on your back and cameras or binoculars around your neck. One gorgeous day can blend into another.

As a photographer I especially relish the golden light of sunrises and sunsets, which never last long enough. I also know from experience that sunny summer days in elk country can suddenly be interrupted by angry storms. More than once I have hurried to lower ground when spectacular electrical storms crackled over the high peaks and meadows. These same storms do not seem to bother elk. I have seen part of a herd continue to graze despite a drenching downpour while the rest remained bedded out in the open, chewing cud, the rain running off the hair of their backs. Another time, dry and warm inside a ranger's cabin, I watched two half-grown elk calves playing and splashing through water puddles formed by the rain that was soaking them. Elk country must be well watered, and summers showers are necessary to keep headwater streams flowing after winter snows have melted.

The same elk country that is normally so pleasant to traverse can become a dreary and seemingly hostile place when the rains last too long. These times are especially difficult when it's necessary to keep cameras and lenses dry in addition to one's self. I have missed shooting interesting elk behavior for fear of damage to valuable equipment.

Summer in elk country tends to be silent, which I suppose can be deafening to a hiker or hunter fresh from the city. Most of the time the only sounds are the sighing of the wind or the song of a stream. Around the edges of forests you might hear the clear whistle of a white-crowned sparrow or the hoarse chatter of a mountain chickadee. During summer none of the larger mammals, including the elk, are very vocal. Bull elk will not be bugling until August comes to an end.

Nights deep in elk country can be still, at times ominously so, especially if you are sleeping alone in a light backpacker's tent. The hooting of great horned owls or the lower-pitched booming call of a great gray owl are only slightly eerie. But too many times the rustle of wind and of brush scraping against tent walls has caused me to sit up in my sleeping bag, suddenly alert, and thinking "grizzly bear." My old friend Gene Wade once noted that there were two kinds of elk country: that with grizzlies and that without. I agreed with him that country "with" was far more exciting.

It has often been claimed that the greatest flower show on earth is scheduled for mid-summer in the Rocky Mountains. The wildflowers reach full bloom in northern New Mexico in June, and the spectacle becomes ever more brilliant as its peak moves northward with the season through Colorado, Wyoming, Idaho, and Montana to Alberta toward the end of July. Look at the map showing elk range in North America and it will also reveal where to find the most colorful native wildflowers.

It is easy to understand why so many sportsmen and -women head for the elk hills and high-country camps every autumn. If it is possible, September and October are even more exquisite than summer. Those lush green meadows have turned to gold, except on frosty mornings when they are a glittering silver in the first rays of the sun. The quaking aspens are now yellow, and some of the leaves are falling. Just as the landscape changes, so do the elk. They are more restless as the first snows begin to fall in the high country. Before long, Peggy and I will be busy waxing our cross-country skis and checking the webbing on our snowshoes. In winter these will be our only means to explore the elk country all around our home.

Wildlife of the Elk's World

Some of the animals that share the elk's world are large, even larger than elk. During my backpacking circuit along the Teton Crest Trail and into a scenic area called Alaska Basin, I met a cow moose crossing a boggy area, followed by a small brown calf. Toward the end of my trip, the darker animal I noticed browsing not far from the trailhead resolved itself into a bull moose in summer's velvet. It suspiciously watched me pass, but otherwise did not move.

Shiras, or Wyoming moose, share much of elk range in the northern Rockies, but are not nearly as abundant. A bull moose in its prime might weigh from fifty to one hundred pounds (22–45 kg) more than an average bull elk, also in its prime. To me the moose is not quite as impressive, as intelligent, or as agile as the elk, but I realize this may be prejudice more than anything else.

Moose probably are not important competitors

Above: The Lamar River Valley, in late November before heavy snows have fallen, is prime elk country in Yellowstone almost the full year around. *Left:* Almost everywhere, elk share their range with mule deer, a smaller member of the family Cervidae. The two species may compete for available food during periods of scarcity. *Overleaf:* From Emigrant Peak and surrounding mountain ranges, herds of elk annually descend into Paradise Valley, Montana, and similar broad valleys in the West to spend winters, often on ranchland.

with elk for food most of the year. Winter might be the exception when wetlands, which moose favor in summer, freeze over and both species are squeezed toward restricted winter range at lower elevations. Peggy and I have watched both browsing heavily, although not close together, on the same willow tracts along the upper Snake River. Biologists tell us that wherever they supply hay during winter emergencies, elk tend to drive moose away.

Another animal that shares elk range almost everywhere in North America is another close relative, the mule deer. During my fall hunting trips years ago, before I traded my rifles for cameras, I would always find the best mule deer bucks when I carried only an elk tag. And one of the finest male elk I ever met, this one at close range, was a harem bull. I found him quite by accident when I was hunting mule deer (and had no elk permit) with bow and arrow in the

rugged Missouri Breaks country of eastern Montana. This bull strolled to within twelve paces of where I crouched on a cold, damp morning. It discovered me and stared in disbelief for several seconds before striding off to follow its cows. Ten minutes later I still felt weak in the knees.

When photographing mule deer, elk are the other large mammals that we most often encounter. The food requirements of the two species are somewhat different—mule deer are more browsers—but both migrate to higher or lower elevations with the seasons. Despite living in numbers in the same environment, it is rare to see the two close together. While bull elk gather herds of cows during the rut, mule deer males court one female at a time. It would be difficult for an elk to keep track of a whole harem in the pine or spruce forest that the muleys prefer.

If you compare the ranges of all five North Ameri-

*Above: Wherever they cling to existence, grizzly bears roam across elk summer range. Some individual bears have learned how to prey upon newborn calves. In spring they also make use of winter-killed elk carcasses. **Facing page, top:** Elk country in Jackson Hole, Wyoming, is shared with the larger moose. Here a cow moose browses for food along the edge of a beaver pond. **Facing page, bottom:** This gray wolf with a ground squirrel in its jaws will normally prey on larger game, such as elk, wherever the two species coexist, as they have for centuries.*

Elk Country and Forest Fires

For far too long we have suppressed natural fires in large tracts of timber, especially in national parks. A predictable result is a vast monoculture usually of lodgepole pine trees, beneath which is dark and almost lifeless ground lacking in bear or elk food. Elsewhere the opposite problem exists. Equally large areas in national forests have been opened up with logging roads and then clear-cut of timber. The regrowth may eventually suit elk if some forest also survives for cover

nearby and if the valuable topsoil is not soon washed away. But the clear-cutting is no boon at all for the bears that do not exist in great numbers anyway. Still, I always think of elk country as also being black bear country.

I had often wondered how elk coped with forest fires, until the great fires of Yellowstone in 1988 when much of the park's old woodlands burned in a series of conflagrations that lasted from mid-summer into late fall. On a number of occasions Peggy and I watched groups of cows grazing in meadows, apparently without concern for the fires raging just beyond them. We watched another herd wade almost leisurely across the Madison River ahead of an advancing wall of flames that seemed to follow them. At the same time television and newspapers daily reported that thousands of elk were being trapped and killed in the fiery holocaust, which they were not.

We were not nearby, however, when the human-caused North Fork Fire of September 9th did encircle and roast alive over three hundred elk on the Blacktail Deer Plateau, ironically only a few days before the first heavy snows of the season fell and extinguished the fire. Later we hiked to the site, which was five miles from the a park road, and counted dozens of white elk skeletons scattered over the black and gray ash. Also dead in the area according to ranger count, were twelve moose, thirty-six mule deer, six black bears and nine bison. Two grizzlies known to live in the vicinity were never seen again.

Although the toll of elk in the 1988 fires did not significantly reduce the park's elk population, it did greatly affect elk winter range, either lightly burning or wiping out large areas. During the winter of 1988–89 many elk that had successfully avoided the fires perished because their winter feeding grounds had been destroyed. Biologists are still (in 1995) debating and trying to assess the long-term effect of the fire on the elk herds.

An elk cow and calf cross the Madison River in Yellowstone to escape the advancing forest fires of 1988. Some elk perished in the widespread blazes.

can deer—family *Cervidae*, including elk, moose, caribou, and mule and whitetail deer—you realize that the range of the elk at least touches the ranges of the other four. It borders whitetail deer country everywhere in the Rocky Mountain foothills and covers woodland caribou country where that species survives in northwestern United States and western Canada.

More than once we have come upon elk in high, precipitous places that seem better suited for bighorn sheep. In western Washington, Olympic elk might climb in summer onto lofty ridges that are the domain of white mountain goats. But next to the mule deer, the other large mammal most likely to be found in elk country is the black bear.

Ursus americanus, the black bear, evolved to exploit roughly the same kind of habitat as the elk: stands of timber mixed with clearings, streamside meadows, lush grasses, and sedges. They are omnivores and often eat dead elk or elk calves. When food runs out in the fall, they hibernate.

In the few mountain ranges where it still survives south of the Canadian border, North America's other bear, the grizzly, also depends on the same range as the elk, at least during the all-important summer months. Grizzlies, like the black bears, are omnivores that can eat anything from moth larvae to carrion, but they normally rely most of all on green grasses and other vegetation for sustenance.

Still, the survival rate of elk fawns is often affected

Above: In the Rocky Mountains, fairy slippers grow beside elk trails in springtime, along with many other exquisite wildflowers. Right: After a late summer thunderstorm, a rainbow glows above important elk range in Montana's Absaroka-Beartooth Wilderness Area.

by grizzly predation. All grizzlies are opportunists that will consume all but the hair and the largest bones of any calf they happen to find. But at least a few adult bears have learned to seriously hunt elk calves (and mule deer fawns) during June. Elk are important to grizzlies at another time, too. When grizzlies leave hibernation dens at the end of winter, green vegetation may not yet have appeared, and many live for a time on winter-killed elk carcasses that are exposed by the melting snows.

One April, within sight of the highway that passes through Silver Gate, Montana, a Yellowstone male grizzly lived, ate, and slept upon the carcass of an elk for more than a week. This source of protein gave the bear a good start for the season, as other winter

Above: The slopes and vicinity of Mount Rainier, Washington, are the picturesque home of elk herds in the Pacific Northwest. Right: Explore almost anywhere in elk country and the large owl you might spot waiting silently in a dead tree snag is a great gray, the largest of all North American owls. Facing page: Cougars, such as this one lurking in Montana, are predators of elk of all ages, but especially of calves and extremely old animals. Occasionally a cougar is killed or injured by its intended prey.

48

kills probably did for grizzlies throughout the park. However, the bear's constant presence kept away the coyotes, ravens, and magpies that were always nearby, vainly hoping to share in the bounty. When it was all over, an amazingly small amount of the elk remained to fertilize the ground where it had died.

In Canada, as well as in northwestern Montana where the species is slowly expanding southward, gray wolves prey on elk of all ages, but mainly on young ones in early summer and on the oldest, weakest adults in winter. Observers in southern British Columbia have long noted that some families of wolves concentrate their elk hunting along certain busy highways where a good many elk are injured or killed by passing cars. Animals in one pack became so bold that they continued to feed on road-killed carcasses even when people in cars stopped to watch or photograph them.

Because they are the most furtive and shy of the

Above: Look for coyotes everywhere in elk range and in all seasons. The song dogs will kill an occasional unguarded calf and in spring will hunt for winter-killed carcasses. Left: Rafts of snow geese are restless over the Tule Elk Refuge marshes where tule elk will wade and drink on hot summer days.

carnivores, we do not readily think of cougars, or mountain lions, as being elk predators. But during his lengthy and thorough examinations of cougars in the central Idaho Wilderness Area, Maurice Hornocker found that this largest of our wild cats could occasionally kill full-grown elk whose movements were hampered by the deep snows of winter. While virtually living with cougars the year around, following and tracking them with hounds, Hornocker also found that cougars could be seriously, even fatally, injured during attacks on elk.

When wandering in elk country, however, a person is much more likely to meet a whole cast of smaller creatures that also have an impact on elk health, nutrition, and longevity. Insect infestations, for example, might be serious enough to drive herds of elk onto higher, windier ridges where the forage is poorer than below, but where they are free of the tormentors. Naturalist Olaus Murie wrote that

sometimes swarms of insects not only determined daily activities and movements of elk, but also accelerated their spring migrations to higher elevations.

I have seen magpies following in the wake of feeding elk and even riding on their backs. One magpie we watched through binoculars in Yellowstone's Mammoth Campground seemed to dig ticks from the ears of a cow that did not resist the delousing. On the other hand, we have watched elk continue to feed as if immune to the hordes of mosquitoes that hovered around them near a bog in Banff National Park, Alberta. These insects were bloodthirsty enough that we ourselves could not remain in the vicinity long enough to photograph the elk.

Elk could probably prosper if there were no ground squirrels at all living in their summer range. But because of the close-cropping feeding habits of the rodents, and the ground fertilized by their droppings, the areas around ground squirrel colonies are

*Above: Following a centuries-old migration route, herds of elk annually pass by this point along Buffalo Creek on the way from southern Yellowstone to winter on the National Elk Refuge near Jackson, Wyoming. **Facing page, top:** Endangered trumpeter swans preen in the Madison River, Montana, as a herd of elk cows with calves is bedded in the meadows not far away. **Facing page, bottom:** The range of the elk ends, in the north, just about where the range of barren-ground caribou, another member of the deer family, begins in Alaska, Yukon, and Canada's Northwest Territories.*

Above: Before the human migration began across America's Great Plains, both bison and elk roamed by the millions. The two still coexist in several American and Canadian national parks. This rutting pair of bison lives on the National Bison Range. **Left:** Elk share parts of their range with bighorn sheep. This ram has descended to the Gardiner River where an elk herd is already wintering. **Facing page:** In golden summer, look for elk cows with calves browsing in forest glades such as this one in Grand Teton National Park, aglow with fireweed.

green and grow more rapidly in early spring than elsewhere, and more than a few elk are able to take advantage of the ground squirrel's behavior.

This next must seem exceedingly strange, if not impossible, and probably is only an aberration. But early in September, well-known wildlife photographers Leonard Lee Rue III and Jim Hamilton watched a cow elk uncover a grassy nest and eat the baby mountain cottontail rabbits inside. Not far from the same spot near Mammoth Hot Springs in Yellowstone, I photographed another, or possibly the same, cow with the quills of a porcupine imbedded in its snout. It is not unusual to find porcupines in elk country, but that does not explain how or why the quills were in the nose. If this was indeed the same elk that ate the baby rabbits, it was surely an unusual animal.

*Above: Serviceberries grow widely in elk country and the animals readily browse on them. **Left:** For a brief period each summer, the high meadows of Beartooth Country along the Wyoming-Montana border serve as summer range for many elk. This land is as spectacular to us as it is important to the animals.*

Elk Behavior

To the Indian, Wapiti was good medicine. Among the tribes he was revered; a symbol
of nobility, pride and passion. He was thought to be endowed with medicinal and romantic powers.
He was credited with the creation of the earth, the power of speech and the ability to summon the
gods and winds for assistance. Warrior societies were named after him. He was seen
in visions and men took their names from him.
—**Dean Krakel II,** *Season of the Elk*

The trail from Dunraven Pass to the summit of Mount Washburn in Yellowstone Park, climbs about 2,000 vertical feet (600 meters) in about three miles. Throughout summer's tourist season it is a popular trail with hikers enjoying the splendid vistas of the surrounding park, the alpine wildflowers, the herd of bighorn sheep ewes with new lambs, and sometimes a grizzly bear passing in the distance. But an intermittent drizzle had discouraged all but a few one morning early in June when I departed the trailhead and began trudging slowly upward, rucksack on my back.

Halfway to the fire lookout on Washburn's peak, I noticed a movement where stunted trees bordered a meadow to the south. Lingering snow from last winter filled a gully nearby. Close to the trees I spotted movement from the corner of my eye. My first thought was "grizzly" because I had seen bears digging for roots in the same area before. But looking through binoculars I saw the bear become an elk cow that was behaving strangely. It was facing upslope and seemed to be swaying and walking slowly in place at the same time, with rear legs widespread. A few seconds later I sat watching the birth of a calf, the only time in a half century of watching the species that I saw this happen.

The cow stood motionless for a few moments after the calf fell, limp, to the ground where it was hidden from view behind a deadfall. But soon she turned about and seemed to be licking the calf and eating the placenta. Perhaps twenty minutes later, through a

Only hours old and barely able to stand, this elk calf nurses for the first time.

drizzle that was turning into a steady rain, I could see that the calf had managed to stand on four wobbly legs. In about an hour, when weather completely engulfed Mount Washburn, and rain was leaking through the seams of my parka, I watched the calf nurse for the first time. Once it lost its footing and toppled over; several minutes passed before it reappeared and was able to suckle again. When my view was completely obscured by the pouring rain, I had to leave the mountain, this time half running downhill, a different trip than I had made, laboring, on the upward trip.

Spring and Summer

Late spring in the northern Rocky Mountains is calving time, a critical period for the elk herds. If the calf crop is normal and more than half of the cows drop calves and half of these calves survive, then the herd can maintain its size. A combination of prolonged foul weather (such as the late arrival of summer) and heavy predation can cause a downturn in regional elk numbers. A good calf crop, plus fair weather and little predation can signal an upswing. Thus a lot depends on the critical April through June season of the elk.

When winter blends into spring, the elk instinctively become restless on their wintering grounds. Biologists have noted that older cows seem to be the most restless, eventually leading the long march, usually upward into higher elevations to follow the retreating snowline. Just behind this line, new green vegetation begins to grow, providing nutrition essential to the elk's survival. The bulls need it to restore fat and muscle to winter-wasted bodies and to grow new sets of antlers, larger than those just discarded. The cows also are thin, but having been impregnated seven months before, need the fresh forage for the calves they carry as well as for themselves.

Almost everywhere, the trek from wintering to calving grounds passes through a landscape that becomes more beautiful every day. Brown is replaced by bright green. Native wildflowers carpet many hillsides. Snow melt fills the many streams that were recently frozen. Without doubt the warm sunshine

is as beneficial to the climbing elk as the sudden abundance of food. At about the same time that arrowleaf balsamroot color the mountainsides yellow from Colorado northward to Alberta, the herds of cows arrive in familiar surroundings, their traditional calving areas. Older females have paused hereabouts in springtimes past, and in fact, most of the herd members were born somewhere in the vicinity. All the bulls are somewhere else, living in bachelor bands. Their wanderings are less predictable and usually take them to higher elevations than those of the females.

Calving areas vary among elk subspecies but most are in evergreen woods mixed with meadows on fairly gentle slopes where there are scattered patches of fairly dense cover. If clear-cut logging has taken place, or there is other human disturbance, the annual calf crop can be greatly reduced. The confused cows are forced to search longer and farther for suitable birthing sites.

Sometime between mid-May and mid-June in the Rockies, the herd cows disperse, usually widely, to individual secluded sites that some sixth sense selects, probably like the site I espied on Mount Washburn. Rarely, two old cows may choose sites not far from one another to calve. Once while hiking near Mammoth Hot Springs in Yellowstone, Peggy and I spotted a cow, shedding and still thin from winter, with a wet newborn calf already up on its feet. As we watched from a distance, the cow not only devoured the placenta and birth membranes, but also seemed to be eating the earth and grass that were saturated with birth fluids. That done, she nursed the calf briefly, bedded, and from that position groomed (by licking) the small spotted young one. Eventually, this cow would leave the calf in that same spot or nearby while she went elsewhere and well out of its sight to feed. It is estimated that about one in every three hundred cows will bear twins rather than single calves.

But why was this cow so fastidious? Most scientists are convinced that it is an ancestral strategy or instinct to protect the calf from carnivores by eradicating any odor that could lead predators to the

Opposite, top: At one month of age, the young elk is able to follow its mother most of the time over their green summer range. Opposite, bottom: Now almost four months old and half-grown, an elk calf still tries to nurse, and will as long as its mother tolerates it. Overleaf: At dusk a cow fords the Madison River in Yellowstone to join its herd and bed down in a grassy meadow overnight.

Above: All-white—albino—calves are a rarity and probably few live very long. This one is probably about two or three weeks old. Right: This bull elk was photographed in June and has the makings of a monster. The enormous velvet-covered antlers still have two months to grow at this point. More than likely the Yellowstone native was poached, since it was never spotted later during the busy rutting season. Opposite: On the sunny morning of a short winter day, an old bull gleans scant nourishment from the coarse grasses under the snow along Montana's Madison River.

newborns. Some ungulate mothers such as bison, musk oxen, moose, and mountain goats aggressively defend young by attacking predators alone or with the aid of herd members. Elk cows rarely and bulls never try to protect young this way. Instead the calves are left alone periodically for a few weeks following the birth while the mothers forage in the distance, probably within hearing, but out of sight. They return only at intervals to nurse the calves, until the young are strong enough to follow them.

For this strategy or rigid discipline to work, the calf, left on its own, must obey instinct and stay immobile no matter how near or how often danger comes. Flattened against the ground, the small animal's light-spotted dark coat helps it blend into its background. I have accidentally found babies hiding this way in what seems an uncomfortable position, and they did not even blink an eye. Still, it was easy to see how such meat-eaters as cougars and coyotes, bears and wolves with much keener senses than mine, would find a certain percentage of every year's elk calf crop.

A calf only comes out of hiding on a signal from its mother: a nasal, high-pitched neigh or mewing. An alarm bark commands the calf to drop back into its prone position immediately. Eventually, about the same time the calf is old enough and physically able to follow its mother and to flee from danger when necessary, mothers and calves gradually rejoin herds summering together on what might be slightly higher range.

During July, August, and into September, adult elk spend about 85 percent of their time eating and the rest of the time resting. Most of the feeding is grazing in open meadows, where, with heads down in grass, all are more vulnerable to predators that they would be if browsing with heads high. But here is the advantage of grouping: At least one of the animals has its head up at any given time and is vigilant, increasing safety for all.

Despite the abundance of food, the sun's warmth, and the daily gamboling, play-fighting, and posturing with contemporaries, a calf's life in its herd is not easy. The calves of dominant cows, the herd leaders, do have advantages, but few cows are ever tolerant of young other than their own. They never will suckle other calves, not even orphans—in fact, they may kick them away. Thus it is important, especially during flight, for a calf to stay close to its mother until this relatively peaceful period changes in September into the most turbulent time of all, the annual rut. By then most calves are able to fend for themselves, and a few female calves may actually be bred.

Fall and Winter

When the rut or breeding season ends, usually in October, life would seem to be all downhill. Because almost everywhere early snows are reclaiming summer ranges, food becomes scarce. The wintering areas lie in valleys far below. Life is also more difficult due to the deepening cold and more intense competition for the shrinking food supply.

At the same time, there is the open hunting season to survive. Keep in mind that even the finest elk country anywhere can support only a limited number of elk. If more than that capacity live on it for long, the environment will be degraded and starvation will follow. In these times of human encroachment and development almost everywhere, and as natural predators are eliminated, legal, regulated hunting is the only practical means to hold elk populations within bounds. No one should mourn the annual harvest of elk, which is actually necessary today for the species as a whole to prosper.

In some parts of the West, whole populations of elk survive the long bitterly cold "hunger moon" on or near feeding grounds that are filled to capacity, where the elk live on rations of hay and vitamin-fortified pellets supplied by people. There are three reasons for the human benevolence: to keep the animals alive for the next hunting seasons, to keep them out of the haystacks meant for livestock, and to maintain the valuable resource they have become in many communities—not only as tourist attractions, but also as a vital part of the ecosystem. Even so, winter

A glittering September frost covers the meadow along the Gibbon River, signaling the onset of the rutting season in Yellowstone Park. This male is not yet mature enough, however, to acquire a harem and to breed.

Studying the Life History of Elk

It is impossible to write about elk behavior without also mentioning the husband and wife naturalist team of Olaus and Margaret "Mardy" Murie who spent a greater part of their lives than any others before or since living with and studying elk. Just after World War I, the U.S. Biological Survey (forerunner of today's U.S. Fish & Wildlife Service) commissioned Olaus to begin a complete study of the life history of elk. This was to include their habitat, migrations, parasites, diseases, food habits, natural enemies, reproduction, and population. It was estimated that this would require five years of hard work.

Actually it lasted fifteen, during which Olaus alone, or with Mardy and their growing family, covered Wyoming, Washington, Montana, Idaho, California, Nevada, Oklahoma, New Mexico, and western Canada. Their central headquarters was in Jackson Hole, just next to the National Elk Refuge. Among many of Olaus's early important discoveries was that winter mortality on the refuge was not necessarily from starvation, but from a sickness called necrotic stomatitis. This disease came from gum lesions caused by eating foxtail hay. When the hay was eliminated, the disease disappeared.

Mardy Murie described to me the fascinating but rugged life that she, their three children, Olaus, and Olaus's aging Norwegian mother led for many summers. They would actually follow the cow elk, setting up camp in the popular calving area near Wyoming's Two Ocean Lake, and then track the herds into the depths of the wilderness. The children were taken from school a month before summer recess so they could share the adventure. Grizzly bears, black bears, and moose were among the "friends" they met. They traveled on foot (their horses' and their own) carrying their camp on mountain pack horses.

One summer the Murie family moved into the luxury of a one-room cabin on the edge of a meadow beside Arizona Creek, near Wyoming's Continental Divide. Mardy remembers reading one evening by candlelight when suddenly she heard a dog barking outside. But they had no dog, and the noisemaker turned out to be a female elk that immediately became silent when Mardy snuffed out the candle. It resumed barking each time the candle was relit. Was

this behavior instinctive?

In the final paragraph of his great book, *The Elk of North America*, published in 1951, Olaus Murie sums up well what he learned during a decade and a half of close observation, and what is still applicable today. "Looking to the future, in view of the needs of the elk and the exacting requirements of recreation based on multiple use, the safest course is to model elk management along natural lines, not only to preserve the elk as a living animal, but also, as far as is reasonably possible, to preserve its distinctive habits as well as its habitat."

Long, cold winters take a terrible toll of the oldest elk, especially of bulls. This could be the final winter for this bull.

can be a grim test for a tough, tenacious species. Elsewhere it is even grimmer and tougher.

Different wild creatures prepare for and cling to life in winter by various means. Many birds migrate. Bears and some other mammals hibernate underground. Others grow heavier or white winter coats. Elk cope in various ways, one of which is saving precious calories and warmth by moving around as little as possible. They also concentrate on south-facing slopes to catch the weak winter sun. When possible they avoid the intense wind chill by moving into timbered areas.

Some of the numerous elk of the Yellowstone ecosystem have one small advantage to dull the edge of winter. They gather around heated thermal areas, often standing close to hot steam vents for warmth. Still this doesn't help much in the season-long struggle against starvation. Elk still must dig and paw in deep snow in search of brown, withered vegetation, and what they find is of low quality. The carbohydrate- and protein-rich grasses of summer store their nutrients underground in winter.

Of course all elk, but especially bulls, are easier targets for predators during the depths of winter. Often they do not have the energy to escape, and deep snows are a greater handicap to the heavier hoofed animals than to their smaller pursuers. Bulls usually enter winter in poorer condition than the cows as the rigors of the rutting season use up all or most of the fat they accumulated during the past summer.

We once watched a large, but emaciated bull die slowly over a period of about ten days on the National Elk Refuge. Already weakened by malnutrition, it became infested with mites, mange, or scabies. Its hair began to fall out and litter the snow wherever it bedded. We noticed that several coyotes seemed to be shadowing this elk, but always keeping a distance until one night when the old bull died. The next morning the coyotes were feeding on the cold, stiff carcass.

Ticks can also be a discomfort, if not a drain on the vitality of wintering elk, particularly where many are crowded together in winter yards. The more animals are crowded together in a space, the more easily parasites and ticks are spread. Ticks can infest elk to such an extent that their snow beds are reddened with their blood; whenever the elk shift position, they crush the ticks that are engorged with elk blood.

During the years that we lived in Jackson Hole and Teton County, Wyoming, where America's largest elk herd winters, we spent many days cross-country skiing in Grand Teton National Park and around the perimeter of the National Elk Refuge. During these travels we met countless elk, and although they are much more tolerant of human approach now, we always gave them a wide berth to avoid stressing them unduly. During March and April, it seemed, we could always sense a subtle change in the big ungulates; as thin and weak as almost all of them were, they seemed to sense that better times were just ahead, that spring was coming.

Old Instincts, New Circumstances

Like all other living species on earth, according to a current, accepted theory, elk behave mostly in obedience to age-old instinct. Over the centuries they have become programmed by heredity to react to certain situations in certain ways. Whenever a set of conditions triggers a response, instinct determines behavior. For example, knowing the best way to find food, how to compete with siblings, avoid predators, and breed. In others words, an elk does not need previous experience or the ability to think to be able to survive. It simply obeys instinct.

But old instincts sometimes collide with new circumstances. The elk's world has changed greatly in just two centuries and drastically in the last hundred years, far too quickly for instinctive knowledge that evolved over thousands of years to keep pace. Some species—coyotes and raccoons and European starlings, for instance—adapt well to changes and to the world crowded by an increasing number of human beings. Other creatures—such as black-footed ferrets, Florida panthers, and California condors—seem unable to adapt at all. North American elk appear to fall somewhere in the middle. They must rely increasingly on learned or acquired behavior patterns to go

*Facing page, top: Some herds of wintering elk—cows, calves, and young bulls—are large, numbering hundreds of animals. This one is near Roosevelt Junction in Yellowstone. Large bulls live separately in small bachelor bands at this time of year. **Facing page, bottom:** Toward the end of the rutting season, this bull and its large harem rest and conserve strength on the relatively warm thermal terraces at Mammoth Hot Springs in Yellowstone.*

along with their instincts.

The theory of obedience to instinct does not seem to be working when elk do the unexpected, often crazy things that we have seen them do. Three Oregon elk hunters spotted a trio of elk, a bull with two cows, walking along a mountain ledge somewhat above them. The men moved ahead for a closer look. Suddenly one of the elk plunged headlong off the cliff and bounced within feet of the hunters on its way to the bottom of the slope. A second elk followed suit in what seemed to be a double suicide. It does not seem that either instinct or learning could have prompted such behavior. But if not, then what did?

I also wonder what triggered another elk into what may be a record journey for the species. When less than two years old, the young bull was fitted by Montana biologist Gary Olson and his helpers with a radio collar for tracking and with ear tag #964. But soon radio contact was lost. The next thing Olson knew, the animal was about 1,800 miles (2,800 km) away in Kansas City, Missouri. For a year or so, people in that vicinity had spotted the animal wandering around. Twice it was hit by cars but walked away apparently uninjured. Eventually workers of the Missouri Department of Conservation tranquilized and live-captured "Big Guy," as he was later known in the Jackson County Park where he was transferred, safe from automobiles, to live with other elk.

Why did Big Guy wander half way across the United States in the first place? As nearly as the journey can be traced, the elk followed the Missouri River eastward. One nature writer joked that the trip was in commemoration of the Lewis and Clark expedition almost two hundred years earlier, although in the wrong direction. Only one thing is certain: Big Guy did not meet any other wild elk along the way. Being of a gregarious species, maybe it just kept searching for company.

Or consider the case of another bull that was live-captured in Yellowstone Park along with about

Its body emaciated from the rigors of the rut, this large old bull seeks food under a weak February sun. It may or may not survive until spring.

twenty-five others. After being tagged, it was transported to a point in central Montana and released almost one hundred miles (160 km) away to restock an area where elk were few. For many years thousands of elk were captured in the park and were shipped away to stock and restock habitat nearby and in at least fifteen other states from Michigan to Washington. But this one bull immediately returned to Yellowstone where it was captured a second time and sent to New Mexico. Here it seemed to be satisfied and survived for almost two years before it was shot by a hunter.

Above: The temperature is well below freezing as Old Faithful erupts beyond these wintering elk in Yellowstone. Only a tough, tenacious species could survive a lifetime of such bitter winters.
Right: Bachelor bulls spar on the wintering grounds near Gardiner, Montana, but now it is more like a friendly greeting than a serious rutting-season rivalry.

*Above: Snow falls on a wintering bull. Later this animal bedded in sagebrush and soon was almost invisible, covered by the blowing snow. Its dense body hair served as insulation against the cold. **Facing page:** Two herd bulls, once rivals, are bachelor friends during the depth of winter, probably increasing security for both.*

Above: A solitary cow finds warmth and a comfortable bed on a winter's day at Opal Terraces of the Mammoth Hot Springs in Yellowstone Park. Many elk winter in this general area, near the park's headquarters. *Left:* A herd of cows and calves march along the slopes beside the Lamar River Valley in Yellowstone, searching for winter forage. The reintroduction of gray wolves into this area in 1995 may affect their future movements and behavior. *Overleaf:* With geysers hissing and steaming in the background, a single elk grazes along the fantastic Firehole River.

Antlers

Elks and deer had traversed the prairie in all directions and trodden many paths to the river. The prairie extended without interruption as far as the eye could reach; it is called Prairie a la Corne le Cerf, because the wandering Indians have gradually piled up a quantity of elks' horns til they have formed a pyramid sixteen or eighteen feet in diameter. Every Indian who passed by makes a point of contributing his part, which is not difficult because such horns are everywhere scattered about; and after the strength of the hunting party is marked with red strokes on the horns they have added to the heap, all these horns of which there are certainly a thousand piled up. The purpose of this practice is said to be a medicine or charm by which they expect to be successful in hunting.
—Maximilian, Prince of Weid, Archduke of Austria, and Emperor of Mexico,
Travels in the Interior of North America, 1832–1834

One gray, cold November afternoon as the 1942 Oregon elk hunting season drew to a close, Opal Evans stepped outside the hunting camp tent where she was cooking the evening meal. Immediately she heard a commotion in the brush nearby and next thing she knew a huge, mad bull elk was bearing down on her. Startled and afraid, Evans locked herself inside a pickup truck parked nearby, until the threatening animal finally left. At dusk her husband Hugh and her brother returned from hunting, and she told them about the encounter.

The next morning and not far away, Hugh shot what almost certainly was that same mad bull. When they broke camp and went home, he tossed the antlers into his barn where they remained unseen for thirty-five years. In 1977, JoAnne Jessel, Hugh and Opal Evans's daughter, was cleaning out the barn and found the antlers. She used the skull as a flower pot and hung the antlers in an oak tree. In 1991, her husband Joe took the antlers to a taxidermist friend, Rich Eckert, who restored and mounted them with a spare cape he had. In 1994, more than a half century after the animal was shot, official Boone & Crockett Club scorer Rusty Linberg measured the head at 418 points. As far as anyone knows, these are the largest elk antlers ever collected in Oregon and among the top ten ever taken in North America.

Every fall the canyons of elk country ring, echoing the shrill, calliope bugling of bull elk. The reverberations are among the most thrilling sounds of nature.

Such stories are not unique. Perhaps better known is the account of John Plute's elk rack. In about 1899, he shot a bull that had monstrous antlers near Crested Butte, Colorado. This rack had seemed to vanish, but it turned up later in the local Elks lodge. But it wasn't until 1962, sixty-three years later, that it was recognized as a world's record for typical elk antlers, which still stands.

A Fascination with Antlers

Male elk have been annually producing and shedding antlers in North America ever since they arrived from Asia. And people have been fascinated—infatuated, really—with elk and their antlers ever since the two species first met. Anything as big and powerful and impressive as a bull with fully grown, polished antlers had to stir reverence among primitive and modern-day hunters alike.

The first explorers who traveled across the northern Great Plains found cairns in the form of large piles of antlers collected by Native Americans. We still do not understand the purpose of these cairns, except possibly to mark trails or as monuments. But we do know that Native Americans everywhere made great and efficient use of discarded elk antlers. From the pure bone material they fashioned everything from charms and crude chisels, to weapons, medicine, and tent pegs.

Late in the twentieth century, we are still making similar use of antlers. As trophies, most antlers are mounted with the whole elk head and hung on home, office, or clubhouse walls for bragging purposes. Antler jewelry for men and women may be more popular now than in early Native American cultures. My friend Glenn Smith crafts exquisite belt buckles of great value from antler coronets in his Billings, Montana, workshop. Today searching for and collecting discarded elk antlers is an absorbing and sometimes profitable hobby for many.

Until recently, vast shipments of antlers were sent to Korea and Taiwan where they were ground up and sold as a cure for everything from baldness and ulcers to arthritis and lost sexual desire. In 1994, elk antlers (without velvet) were bringing from five to seven dollars per pound on the Oriental market. That helps explain why the Wyoming Game & Fish

Department reported a rash of antler thefts across the state from residences, private businesses, national parks, saloons, and even from their own offices. About four hundred pounds (180 kg) were stolen from the G&F compounds in Jackson, and two hundred pounds (90 kg) disappeared one night from the Cody office.

Many state record and near-record antlers were taken on tour around the United States in 1994. Roger Selner of Livingston, Montana, collected the large antlers and displayed them in a travel trailer that he tows to hunters' and conservation meetings, sponsored by *Eastman's Journal*, a trophy-hunting magazine. In Selner's collection are the all-time, largest-known elk antlers, taken in 1961 near Gilbert Plain, Manitoba. This is a non-typical rack that happens to be of the Manitoban subspecies and scores 447 1/8 Boone and Crockett points. Selner also owns the largest shed antlers, picked up by a lucky hiker in Montana's Cabinet Mountains in 1980.

The Necessity of Antlers

Antlers are a means of recognition and status in a herd. Maybe as important as the size of antlers is how well the bull displays them, by raising, lowering, and twisting his head. The larger the antlers, the more conspicuous, the more majestic the bull appears in a group of elk. In winter antlers can be the means to monopolize or take over a critical food source from other elk. But by far the greatest value of antlers is most obvious soon after the velvet peels away and the rutting season begins in glorious September. That's when they advertise a bull's availability to his harem of cows.

Scientists generally agree that forty different species and perhaps five times that many subspecies of deer inhabit the globe. Altogether they comprise the family *Cervidae*, which is distinct from almost all other creatures in that the males grow and discard antlers every year. The only exceptions are the Chinese water deer and the musk deer of Asia that grow tusks instead of antlers. An elk cow with fully developed antlers once spent a winter on the National Elk Refuge, but this is both rare and a curiosity.

Antlers are the fastest bone growth known to science. A healthy, mature male elk can acquire a rack

Photographed in mid-July, this Alberta bull already wears impressive antlers. With another month of growth yet to come, it will be a strong competitor in the September breeding tournaments.

weighing thirty-five to forty pounds (15–18 kg) in just four and a half months. They are cast or shed about nine months after growth begins.

Although antlers are too often mistakenly called horns—as in the Elkhorn Bar or Elkhorn Creek—the two should not be confused. Horns of wild sheep, musk oxen, wild goats, and antelope are composed of keratin, the same material as hooves, claws, and fingernails. Horns grow for as long as the animal lives. Except with American pronghorn antelope, horns are permanent, never forked (as are antlers), or shed.

Elk antlers (as well as other types of antlers) grow from pedicles, which are twin bony protuberances of living tissue on top of the skull. The eventual size of a bull's rack is limited to a great extent by the size or diameter of the pedicles at birth. The angle of placement of the pedicles on the skull determines whether the antlers will have a wide spread, stand high, or strike a balance.

Above: Now as summer blends into fall, the velvet peels or is scraped away from the antlers of bull elk. The rutting season is at hand. **Left:** *Few elk ever reach the dimensions of this bull in Waterton National Park, Alberta. Although massive, its antlers are almost dwarfed by its great body size.*

Above: In frustration, irritation, or perhaps in a show of power, bull elk sometimes spar with saplings, even uprooting them. Small trees freshly stripped of bark are signs of rutting elk in the vicinity. *Left:* Although of pure, hard bone, antlers sometimes snap when elk bulls lunge head to head in combat. This one lost both a contest with a larger bull and half its crown at the same time. *Facing page:* This bull is one and a half or two and a half years old, with small antlers, and will not be a factor in the approaching mating season. Full maturity arrives at about five and a half years of age.

The male sex hormone, testosterone, plays the major role in an elk's antler cycle. Testosterone levels are never constant in any wild deer, including elk, but rather rise and fall seasonally in response to increasing or decreasing lengths of daylight hours, a biological response known as photoperiodism.

Antler growth starts in springtime, around late April, soon after the old set is cast, when the testosterone level is low and the bulls are not fertile. Growth continues through summer as testosterone increases to a peak in September, which brings on the rut and breeding season. The hormone level begin to fall in late December, and when it reaches its lowest level, from February into early April, the shedding of antlers is triggered.

Age and possibly health also have an influence on shedding. Older, stronger males are the first to shed (at times in January) while some spikes or yearlings may not lose theirs until as late as May. For the record, one of the largest bulls we have ever photographed, and which seemed to be in poor physical condition, still carried its antlers in early March, following a fair, mild Wyoming winter.

On a number of occasions in late winter, we have seen bulls carrying only one antler. But most often both antlers are dropped the same day, if not actually within an hour or less of one another. Once we watched an elk with only a single antler stand and shake its head violently until the antler was finally tossed aside. Through binoculars we could clearly see both the bloody pedicle and the reddened butt of the fallen antler.

Antler development is pretty well programmed before birth. Pedicles appear on the tiny skull even while the bull calf is carried in its mother's womb. Small cowlicks on the forehead are the first sign of pedicles in newborn calves, and antlers first appear when the calf is a year old. The speed of growth and the eventual mass of the antlers increase with each passing year if nutrition remains adequate, until the animal reaches its prime usually between five and one-half and seven and one-half years of age. After that, growth and mass begin to decline.

To date there is no general agreement on why elk cows do not have antlers. In fact questions still re-

A herd bull patrols the stream bank that serves as the boundary of its harem in Yellowstone.

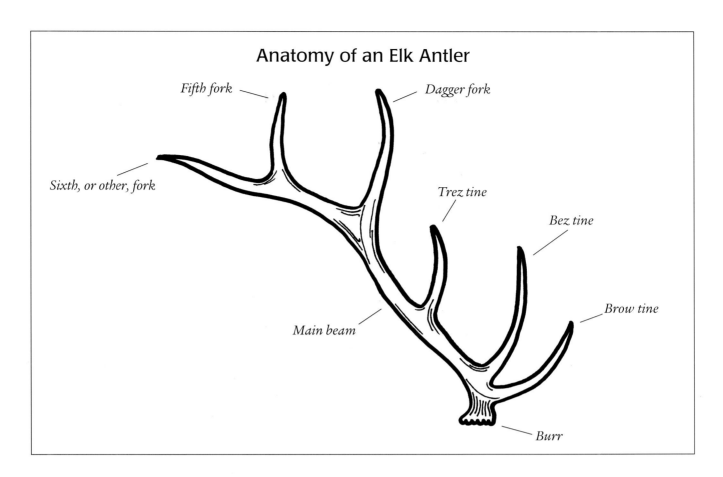

Anatomy of an Elk Antler

Fifth fork

Dagger fork

Sixth, or other, fork

Trez tine

Bez tine

Brow tine

Main beam

Burr

main as to exactly why bulls do grow them. They are not a means of defense against predation as always believed; both sexes use speed afoot and kicking with their front hooves for that purpose. Also, many bulls have already cast their antlers at the time when they might most need them for defense, before bitter winter fully gives way to spring.

Throughout growth, all antlers are covered with a brown skin that looks fuzzy, feels like suede to the touch, and is called velvet. This velvet is really a modified extension of the skin on a bull's head and is sensitive. Like the whiskers of a fox or wild cat, the short velvet hairs help warn of obstacles in the elk's path, thereby preventing injury to eyes and to the developing antlers. In autumn when the antlers are fully formed, the blood vessels nourishing the velvet at the base of the antlers die, and the velvet peels away, or it may be scraped off. The antler has stopped growing and hardens. The bare antler now is smooth and tough enough to withstand the considerable impact when it clashes head to head with another bull during combat in the rut.

Antler Dimensions

Like human fingerprints and the patterns of a leopard's spots, no two sets of elk antlers are exactly alike in weight, mass, or shape. Antler dimensions or the number of points is never an indication of the bull's exact age, which can only be determined by a close examination of the teeth.

A young bull's first set of antlers is normally not branched and resemble drumsticks. They are called spikes. The second year, it may have two or three points per side. Three to five points per side are likely for a third set, and up to what is known as a "royal," with six points on each side.

Males with twelve points or more are almost always in the true trophy class. I have seen two elk with a total of fifteen points, seven on one side, eight on the other. One of these was in Yellowstone Park and still in the velvet; it was poached not long afterward. The other was a Roosevelt elk in Olympic National Park, Washington.

Nowadays you are most likely to find huge racks among bulls that spend their lives entirely in national

Showing its heavy, trophy-size antlers to advantage, a bull announces its arrival or presence to all other elk in the area.

Antler Measuring Systems

Over the years a number of different systems have been devised to measure, grade, and compare the antlers and horns of all big-game animals. But the best, most equitable, and most widely accepted method in North America today is that devised by the Boone & Crockett Club, now based in Missoula, Montana.

By the Boone & Crockett Club's method, an elk bull's antlers are carefully measured in inches, down to one-sixteenth of an inch. The measurements are then added together, the total being the sum of the following dimensions: the lengths of the two main beams, the lengths of all tines, the greatest inside distance between the two antler beams, and the largest circumference of the main beams above the coronet. The total is the preliminary score.

If it is a typical head, with the opposing antlers being symmetrical or nearly so, points (inches) are deducted for any abnormal points, to reach the final score. Non-typical (non-symmetrical or malformed) heads are scored in the same way: all tines or points are measured no matter how irregular or where they are located, and no deductions are made in determining the final score. Hence non-typical racks usually have higher scores than typicals.

In 1932, the Boone & Crockett Club published its first *Records of North American Big Game.* The tenth and most recent edition was

The rut has ended and for this bull a long winter of thin rations and cold days lies ahead. It will drop, or cast, those fine, wide-spreading antlers in early April.

printed in 1993, and includes the scores of all the largest known elk racks, typical and non-typical. Safari Club International of Tucson, Arizona, recognizes a similar scoring system and publishes an *International Record Book of Trophy Animals,* which recognizes the largest elk taken by its many members.

parks, rather than outside such sanctuaries. Where they are hunted, especially where hunting pressure is heavy, bulls are less likely to live long enough to reach their maximum potential antler growth.

In a prime bull, the main antler beams or arms may grow four and one-half feet (135 cm) long or more. The first forks on each side are known as the brow tines, the second are bez tines, and third are trez tines. Next, and often the longest forks, are called

daggers. After that are the fifth and sixth or other forks. Occasionally the dagger tine will fork or there will be a terminal fork, which might be a sign of interbreeding with red deer. In typical heads, the brow tines grow nearly parallel with the tips curved slightly upward. Bez tines of good specimens are as long or longer than the brow tines. The largest known Roosevelt elk, from the Tskia River region of British Columbia, had nineteen points, or tines.

This meeting of young bulls may be more a noisy shoving match than a savage duel for dominance and a harem.

The Rutting Season

After a while the wild music comes again—a low, throat-clearing tremolo stretching into a taut alto, wavering up to a soprano vibrato and sustaining, then trailing off rapidly in pitch and volume like a cry carried away on the wind; the finale is a staccato triad of sharp coughs. No mistaking that voice. It's the big red bull heralding the onset of autumn.
—David Petersen, *Among the Elk*

Early September is an absolutely magical and exciting time in Alberta's Jasper National Park. Most of the summer's tourists have retreated home to the cities. Leaves of deciduous plants are changing color to yellow and gold. The weather tends to be clear, invigorating, and cool. The alpine scenery of autumn in Jasper compares with any in the Canadian Rockies or anywhere else. The shrill bugling that reverberates across open meadows and along river edges is the sound of Jasper's elk population in full rut. It is prime time in the life cycle of the species, as well as the best time to be out in the field watching them.

Before dawn one foggy fall morning, Peggy and I were eating breakfast and reloading cameras in Jasper's Whistler Campground when we first noticed blue shadows moving quietly in the dim light just outside our van. The shadows were a harem of cow elk being herded aggressively by a huge bull that bellowed and pawed the ground in passing. It was an eerie, almost frightening experience there in the foggy half-light. Despite the fact that we have been photographing elk for many Septembers, in many different places, we found ourselves remaining motionless and silent as the group passed.

By the time breakfast was finished the entire herd had vanished into the gloom, so we drove a few miles toward where the park road paralleled the Athabasca River just beyond Jasper Townsite. The light was much brighter now, and we had brief glimpses of the dark current where the fog thinned and lifted. In one such opening we spotted another harem

Another bull has bugled far in the distance, and this powerful animal is responding, no doubt with a message to stay far away.

of fifteen cows, followed by a male even larger than the campground bull. From a distance we watched them all plunge into the cold, swift water and then come directly toward us, struggling to keep from being swept downstream. All managed to emerge dripping onto a gravel bar in mid-river. The bull bugled at intervals, even when belly-deep in the river. We can only guess what happened next because the fog closed in again, obscuring our view.

We realized then that two, not just one, bulls were bugling out in the void; we had only seen the one. As we strained to hear better, the calling stopped and then came the loud crash of antlers. Then silence, followed in a few minutes by the regular bugling of just one bull. When the overcast was finally dissolved by the sun at mid-morning, the entire harem was still on the same river bar where we had last seen them. But now all were bedded down and most seemed to be dozing. Only the bull was still on its feet, staring toward a river bend downstream. There, through our binoculars, we could see the rival bull, slashing at brush with its antlers. It was an exciting morning we would never forget.

The Rutting "Tournament"

Wyoming natural history writer and editor Chris Madson described the elk rut as "an odd combination of courtly tradition and brute force." Author Byron Dalrymple states that the rutting bull is a sultan and a classic male chauvinist. Both are right on target.

From the observer's standpoint, the annual rut resembles a tournament in which all the males compete at least briefly for the right to breed. The younger, smaller ones are eliminated almost immediately. They are left to spar with one another out on the fringes of the main action. Mostly by posturing, maneuvering, patrolling, and bugling, the most powerful and persistent bulls eventually emerge as the most successful harem builders and so will do nearly all the breeding. The aim of the game is to acquire as many cows as possible and then to maintain them through the entire rutting period. It is never an easy task.

It is interesting that throughout the rutting period cows seem little impressed with male activities all around them. They alternately graze, bed down to rest, and allow themselves to be herded around. If any are greatly impressed by the bugling, it isn't noticeable.

Unlike the cows, bulls eat little during the breeding period that averages a month long. Mornings and afternoons are the times of greatest activity. If the number of eligible bulls in the region is high, constantly threatening to take a portion of the cows, a harem bull has almost no respite during the period.

Occasionally a cow will try to wander away, but an energetic harem bull immediately cuts off the escape and retrieves the wayward cow. It seems to me that bulls like to select large meadows where streams can act as barriers or boundaries, and where it is easier to keep an eye on both the females and any of the hopeful males that continually stalk the fringes, ever alert for an available cow. It is difficult work that takes a considerable physical toll, and it is not at all unusual to find bulls that are exhausted when the first snows of October begin to fall.

Throughout the rut, the seven-hundred-pound-plus (300-kg-plus) bulls urinate often on their bellies, hocks, and necks, soaking themselves with a musk that even humans can smell from some distance away. Sourced from preorbital glands next to the eyes, bulls also rub this musk and scent on vegetation to advertise their presence. Scent is also left on saplings that are slashed with the bulls' antlers. Some bulls excavate shallow wallows in damp soil and urinate in these; they then plaster themselves by wallowing in the muck. The end product is a raunchy, foul-smelling, mud-caked, noisy, wild-eyed critter with rolling eyes and a wet nose, more than ready for action.

There is an old and widely held myth about the elk rut, or breeding season. Old-timers and hunting outfitters have assured me that unseasonably hot weather delays the rut and that an early cold spell can hasten the activity. But the fact is that hot or cold weather have little bearing on the timing of the rut. Instead this period is determined by photoperiodism, the biological influence of the length of daylight and darkness. Every year at a certain latitude, the length of daylight hours diminishes at about the same date, triggering hormonal changes in elk and most other American hoofed species. Instinctively the elk bulls begin to collect cows that will soon come into estrus, and merge the cows into harems. At the same time, the fellow bachelor bulls with which they

Above : *A bull stands close guard over a trio of bedded cows. One or more of these is probably coming into estrus.* **Overleaf:** *In Gibbon Meadow, Yellowstone, the cows of a small harem seem to show little interest in the macho antics of a bugling bull.*

Elk copulation takes place only when the female is ready, and then is brief. Moments after this peak photo, both were otherwise occupied, the cow feeding, the bull bugling.

have peacefully spent the summer become rivals.

During typically cool Septembers, elk are active from dawn to dusk in open meadows white with frost in early mornings. During an extremely hot and dry September, however, the rut may *seem* to be delayed—at least it is more difficult to observe. Most likely this is because the animals are less active during the day, preferring to rest in the cool shade and then become active after dark. More than once when camped in the high country during exceedingly hot Septembers, I have been entertained by bulls bugling and stomping around all night long.

Some seasons the rut seems to end abruptly. I recall a time in late September when Yellowstone's Elk Meadow was alive with animals, and bugling could be heard well after sunset. In fact some bugling lasted all night long. The next morning only a few cows waded into the Gibbon River and then disappeared into lodgepole pine timber in the distance. Light rain turned to sleet and finally to heavy snow. Then and for months to come, the whole scene was silent and empty.

Other years the rut seems to wind down slowly. Daily the bulls seem less and less active, with some bordering on exhaustion. Rather than stand, the bulls bugle while bedded, and less often. The cows, almost all of them bred, begin to move away from the rutting meadows in search of better browsing elsewhere, often to lower altitudes. Compared to a few weeks earlier, the scene is lifeless and dreary.

One morning near Norris Junction in Yellowstone, as breeding activities had almost ended, we watched some strange elk behavior. A bull was bedded in tall, rank grass with its face flat out on the ground. For some time an old cow kept poking at the bull's rump with its front hooves until the bull finally had to stand up. Once on four feet, the cow persisted in nudging the unresponsive male, finally trying to mount him. He was apparently totally uninterested, and we have always wondered if the cow's message here was that the rut wasn't really finished—at least not for the cow.

After copulation, the bull moves on, looking for other mating prospects.

The harem bulls pay a stiff price for their seasonal role of dominance. Their odds of living through the upcoming winter may not be as high as for some lesser bulls that are in better physical condition. But the bloodlines of the harem bulls will survive in future generations of elk.

The Role of Bugling

An elk's bugling is a form of male advertising during the rut. Most biologists agree with well-known Canadian animal behaviorist Valerius Geist that by bugling loud and often, the bulls try to "out-advertise" rivals and attract more females to their group. Bugling almost certainly is not a challenge to combat as often stated.

Studies of the elk's cousin in Europe, the red deer, which roars rather than bugles to advertise during the rut, have revealed that red deer bulls that roar most frequently with the greatest intensity or volume are most successful in the breeding game. That might also be true with elk, but not all researchers who have studied them in North America agree.

Elk bugling, if bugling is really the best word, is unlike any other sound in nature. It begins as a low rasp, rises and becomes more shrill as the bugler stretches its neck and opens its mouth. The scream then climbs over several octaves and drops off quickly into a series of harsh coughs or grunts. At close range it is almost a hair-raising sound, even terrifying, when heard close up for the first time. But in the distance it has a much different, almost bell-like, siren quality.

There is also the often-repeated myth that the size and age of a bull elk can be determined by the volume and sound of its voice. While it is true that yearling bulls can certainly be distinguished from much older individuals in that way, the bugling of a modest-sized four- or five-pointer might penetrate and carry over the foothills as far as the call of a bull with the largest rack in the Rocky Mountains. Or maybe not. Volume is not in direct proportion to age, body, or antler size.

I recall one fine bull that commanded a harem of some twenty females one September in Yellowstone Park's Gibbon Meadow. This vast plain, bisected by the meandering Gibbon River, has long been one of the finest sites to study the antics of rutting elk. Judging from its great size, heavy antlers, and almost arrogant attitude, this was an old bull perhaps in its sixth or seventh season. But its voice was barely a croak. It would prance, drive other bulls far away, urinate on its hooves, tear up turf with its antlers, and then raise its antlers to advertise prowess. As the last days of the rut ran out at the end of September, and some of the harem cows, already bred, were beginning to drift away, almost no sound at all came from the old bull's throat. Despite his deficiency, this bull remained undisputed chieftain during the entire period of the rut, showing, apparently, that bugling may not be a major factor in breeding success.

Rutting Duels

Wildlife artists like to paint pictures of great bull elk facing one another or locked head to head in savage combat. Such scenes really do occur, although not often. Over many years, I have seen large bulls seriously fighting only a few times, and it was always a no-holds-barred, ruthless contest. I have often read that bulls defending harems are not programmed to injure one another, that they only mean to drive the rival away. But I have seen just enough battles to know this is false.

Antlers play a most important part in the competition. Smaller, younger bulls immediately recognize a superior head and avoid the animal carrying it. Most of the visible violence during the rut occurs when bulls of nearly equal prowess meet.

Most fights are settled quickly, once and for all, when the loser suddenly breaks off and runs away.

Midday during the elk rutting season in Alberta's Jasper National Park. These cows are bedded down beside the Athabasca River. The bull is testing—tasting—the air for signs of estrus in his harem. **Overleaf:** *During the last days of the rut, a thoroughly tired bull elk rests briefly in the late September sunshine as his cows wade in the Gardiner River.*

The winner always follows to make sure it runs far enough. But as long as the head-to-head shoving and thrusting with antlers lasts, the clear aim, it seems to me, is to kill. Consider the following early September incident in Banff National Park, Alberta.

Dave Yoder of Ohio was enjoying the last day of his vacation, video camera in hand, when he joined a throng of Banff Townsite residents and fall tourists at a picnic and playground at the edge of town. Two large bull elk decided to join the party as well. When the rutting bulls began to fight amid the slides and swingset, the crowd scattered, parents frantically herding their children to safety. Everyone watched in fascination and horror as the antlers of one of the bulls became entangled in the stout chains of a swing, leaving it helpless to fight its rival. But there was no mercy. The rival repeatedly attacked, plunging its antlers into the flanks and face of the trapped bull

until it sagged, dead, in a bloody heap, still entangled in the chains. Dave Yoder got all of it on videotape. Professional cameraman, Joey Olivieri, also photographed the grisly incident.

Many years ago I was photographing two bulls battling beside the Madison River in Yellowstone Park. One stumbled and before it could recover, was speared repeatedly by the other before it broke through an undercut bank and fell into the Madison. The winner of this bout continued to follow the badly injured loser as a strong current swept it downstream. These incidents seem to illustrate that bulls will indeed pursue rivals well past the point where they are no longer a threat to the harem, even to and past the point of death.

Another interesting facet is that during the bulls' duel beside the Madison River, several cows remained close to the combatants, uninterested in the

*Above: A bull stands guard over his harem of cows, keeping watch for younger bulls that may try to encroach on his territory. **Facing page, top:** There is evidence that a bull's stature or dominance may depend on the frequency or volume of its bugling. Not all observers agree this is true, however. **Facing page, bottom:** These young bulls are battling beyond the area staked out by a much larger harem bull. They are practicing for the main event next year, or perhaps the year after that.*

battle. In our photographs, all of the females have their heads down, feeding peacefully, despite the violence going on all around them.

Occasionally the antlers of battling elk become locked together, although this probably does not happen as often as with whitetail deer. Back-country outfitter Gene Wade once found a locked pair in the Beartooth Mountains northeast of Yellowstone. One of the bulls was dead and the other could barely open an eye when Wade came upon them. Wade could only guess how long the two had been locked together—probably at least a week. He was unable to separate them, but on his return trip, only ten days later, found only the antlers and scattered bones. There were tracks and dung of coyotes and a grizzly bear all around. It is doubtful if any elk ever survive having their antlers firmly entangled.

The arena for this sparring match is a slough of the Athabasca River. The bulls were still rattling antlers when a September rain began to fall twenty minutes later.

*Above: Although the volume and tone of an elk's bugle may be some indication, at least to human listeners, of the animal's age, this is not a reliable indicator. Nevertheless, many people believe a deeper call comes from an older bull. **Facing page, top:** An early overnight snowfall does not dampen the rutting activities near Roaring Mountain in Yellowstone. Here a harem bull clashes with a persistent rival, which was eventually driven away. **Facing page, bottom:** With a watchful eye on a smaller bull loitering in the distance, a harem bull patrols the area he has staked out.*

Above: Portrait of an exhausted bull elk. This one has been running ahead of the advancing Yellowstone forest fires and rutting at the same time. *Right:* A cow, past estrus and having mated, is restless and tries to drift away unseen to a better foraging area.

When winter finally ends, all elk shed their winter coats, and bulls cast their antlers. This large male, although thin, has survived to greet another spring.

Elk and Humans

Like winds and sunsets, wild things were taken for granted until progress began to do away with them. Now we face the questions whether a still higher "standard of living" is worth its cost in things natural, wild and free. For us of the minority, the opportunity to see geese is more important than television, and the chance to find a pasque-flower is a right as inalienable as free speech.
—Aldo Leopold, *A Sand County Almanac*

For more than a century, Gardiner, Montana, has been associated with elk and elk hunting as much as with being the busy, main, northern gateway to Yellowstone National Park, which immediately adjoins the town. Throughout the early 1900s, small armies of hunters arrived via the Northern Pacific railroad to go hunting in the surrounding mountains from before Thanksgiving until March. The hunters pitched tent cities in the sometimes deep snow just north of Gardiner, and all lodgings were always full. They had plenty of game to hunt.

The trains, historian Doris Whithorn relates, resembled arsenals heading south and mobile packing plants on the return trips. Carcasses of elk were piled high on flatcars and in boxcars. Any hunters who were unlucky or poor shots and failed to shoot their own elk could buy one for four or five dollars, or even for a couple of drinks at the bar. Over the decades, these annual late-season hunts have become famous—great adventures, notorious or scandalous, depending on your viewpoint.

For many years the Gardiner hunt was little more than a shooting gallery, a dangerous front-line affair that came to be known as The Firing Line. The targets were herds of elk migrating northward out of Yellowstone toward centuries-old wintering areas. Emerging from the national park, animals were ambushed along the way, pretty much without regulation. To avoid disappointment, many hunters shot several elk, knowing that more than one would be claimed by other hunters. And some of the shooters were themselves shot.

Many sportsmen regard the North American elk as the world's top antlered trophy. Only mature moose and caribou bulls sometimes carry heavier racks.

For several years in the early 1950s, the hunt began when gunners gathered en masse near a mining complex at Jardine, a few miles from Gardiner, and awaited a siren or whistle blown at 8 A.M. At the same time, a gate at Eagle Creek was opened, and hunters in cars, on horseback, and afoot then charged up the road and began shooting as soon as they saw the elk. During one wintry day in January 1946, an estimated 1,800 elk were shot before noon. The carnage was successful in harvesting surplus elk from the great herds that spent summers in Yellowstone Park, but it was more anarchy than ethical big-game hunting as we know it now. One early writer called it "sanctioned insanity." The only requirements for the hunt were a train ticket, a red cap, and an inexpensive license or game tag.

One often-repeated story describes well the Gardiner hunting. Almost all of the hunters were male, but one day a female star of the Hollywood silent movies arrived incognito among the train passengers. She insisted on hunting in her full-length, heavy fur coat and fancy shoes; so encumbered, she fell down and floundered in deep snow. Wrapped in fur, she looked like a downed elk, and the story goes that four hunters tagged her before she could regain her footing.

Some hunters practically made careers of elk hunting in this area of south-central Montana. One hunter, William Hruza, built a waist-high fence around his house and lot on Third and Yellowstone Streets in Livingston with the antlers of about 150 bulls. Taxidermists did well, too, although trophy antlers were not as coveted then as now.

In April 1903, President Theodore Roosevelt visited Gardiner and Yellowstone Park. A reporter for the *Livingston Enterprise* wrote that during one excursion in the park, the presidential party encountered one herd of 2,000 elk. Before departing, our first (and only, it seems) chief executive with a genuine, passionate interest in conservation, gave a bully speech as he dedicated the stone-arch gate still used by millions to enter Yellowstone. "I have been literally astounded at the enormous quantities of elk," Roosevelt said, "and I hope they will be observed by our children and their children's children."

The hunts and hoopla ended temporarily in 1968 when the elk population crashed and a total of only one hundred animals were bagged by many times that number of hunters. The crash probably was caused by the combination of too much hunting for far too long, coupled with a series of cold and devastating winters.

Living with Elk

One morning in late October 1994, an old cow elk wandered through the stone arch that Teddy Roosevelt had dedicated, passing from Yellowstone Park right into Gardiner. There it began to graze on the coarse grass growing along a boundary fence just across the street from Cecil's Restaurant. Several tourists paused to watch the unusual scene and somehow a tiny white poodle with a red jingle-bell collar escaped from one of them. It ran, yipping and snarling, toward the elk, which paid no attention. More people gathered.

"If elk were good for anything a-tall," a local cowpoke standing nearby commented to me, "that cow would crush the skull of that crummy little dog."

The checkout lady in the local grocery was also on the scene when the cow finally walked away, and the owner retrieved his poodle. "These elk are a danger to our children," she said, "and they poop everywhere."

Maybe more than anywhere else, the people of Gardiner have a love-hate relationship with the elk that invade their town every fall and often overstay their welcome. Among the places they poop—and where whole herds often graze and bed down—is on the high school football field. It is never necessary to either fertilize the ground or mow the grass here. This may be the only town in America where elk regularly watch the football team and cheerleaders practice from the sidelines. A lot of residents do not welcome them, and in fact are afraid of the big deer. A man walking home late one night after a party at a local saloon stumbled over an elk sleeping in the street, and was kicked in the behind and elsewhere. He has walked with a limp ever since and has few

Facing page, top: Spoils of an elk hunt in Gardiner, Montana, in 1906. (Courtesy Park County Museum) Facing page, bottom: Gardiner, Montana, was the elk-hunting capital of the world in the early 1900s. Proud of the spoils from the 1906 hunt, elk hunters, Northern Pacific railroadmen, and the town's women and children pose at the Gardiner train station with carcasses and trophy heads being shipped back East. (Courtesy Park County Museum)

good things to say about elk. I once saw a bull rubbing its rump against a pickup truck parked near the town post office, trapping the driver inside.

But not all Gardiner residents resent the elk. Many motels, cafés, and other businesses that might otherwise close when the main tourist season ends about Labor Day, now remain open and busy accommodating a whole corps of nature photographers and elk hunters that descend upon the area. It is an understatement to say that elk guarantee a good bit of income and more than a few jobs in Gardiner. The owners of the Flamingo Motor Lodge pass out picture postcards showing a herd of elk relaxing on their front lawn. A waitress at the Town Café told me, "They stink, but most of us welcome them anyway."

The small community of government employees at Mammoth Hot Springs, the headquarters of Yellowstone Park, just south of Gardiner, has a similar problem every fall. Meghan Keigley had just celebrated her sixth birthday and was watching a bull elk on the front lawn through a picture window of her home in Mammoth Hot Springs. The animal suddenly whirled, bellowed, and charged the window with ears laid back and antlers forward. It might have crashed through the window except that the antlers caught on an overhanging eave, which splintered and stopped the charge. Quite likely this animal was attacking its own reflection in the glass, mistaking it for a rival bull.

Jean Neutzel has lived in Mammoth Hot Springs for seventeen years and is secretary to the park superintendent. Once in late September, she was walking home for lunch when a herd of six cows followed by an agitated bull crossed her path. When the bull saw her, it lost interest in the cows and chased her. Fortunately Neutzel is used to the autumn madness and has been pursued before, so she is swift afoot. She simply scrambled up a hill and put a stout tree between herself and the elk, which abandoned the chase and returned to his cows.

Unlike in Gardiner, which they only visit every fall and winter, the elk live year around on the lawns and among the buildings of Mammoth Hot Springs. Most of the time they are more of a tourist attrac-

Above: An elk hunt into the Canadian or American Rockies can be an adventure of a lifetime. Here a hunter and guide in the Teton Wilderness of Wyoming look down on a mountain meadow where they have heard a bull elk bugling. Facing page: A pack string of hunters and guides ride out from a trailhead to a base camp high and deep in the Teton Wilderness.

tion than a nuisance. But come September, according to one resident, the otherwise quiet community changes into a "lust-filled cauldron of bubbling elk hormones." Males are fighting, crashing antlers, and kicking up turf and dust. Miraculously, no resident has ever been severely injured, although the potential is certainly there. Principal John Whitman of the Yellowstone elementary school in Mammoth Hot Springs has counted as many as fifty elk on the playground just outside the classrooms. One day a pair of bulls broke up a recess softball game and began sparring between the pitcher's mound and third base. Students regularly have to clean elk droppings from their shoes before coming indoors.

Fisheries biologist Lynn Kaeding was walking to work one morning with pressing matters on his mind when he heard raucous laughter coming from his office windows. His coworkers were watching the young bull that was following, unknown to Kaeding, right in his footsteps. Kaeding stopped suddenly in fear of an attack. But the elk, having apparently taken a liking to him, only licked the back of his neck. Smiling friends thought it was attracted by his after-shave lotion rather than his charm. For the most part, the people of Mammoth Hot Springs are tolerant of "their" elk. Nothing generates more conversation, much of it humorous, than their big four-footed friends.

Elk and Civilization

Unfortunately elk aren't welcome or even tolerated everywhere in the West as they usually are in Gardiner. Consider the too-typical case of rancher Ben Hurwitz who owns 10,000 acres in the southern foothills of the Little Belt Mountains near White Sulphur Springs, Montana. Hurwitz claims he developed ulcers from watching about four hundred animals invade his land every winter and eat too much of the grass that might otherwise fatten his cattle. In 1993, he sold enough timber from his place to erect an eighteen-mile (29-km), seven-foot-high (2-m), twelve-strand elk-proof super fence that almost encircled his property. He figured the barrier would pay for itself in ten years because now he can

Whether photographing, hunting, or just watching, the great moment comes when a bull such as this one appears on the magnificent mountain scene.

add two hundred head of cattle to his herd of six hundred (at a time when beef consumption is generally declining in the United States).

The impact of the fence is predictable, and other ranchers in the area and elsewhere too may be tempted to copy it. Biologist Dick Bucsis of the Montana Department of Fish, Wildlife and Parks, points out the obvious: Fences such as this will severely reduce the elk's winter range in the region. Further fencing might well eliminate elk altogether from the Little Belt Mountains because it is vital that the animals have a place to live in the winter.

Make no mistake that under certain conditions elk can be troublesome, even dangerous, when their numbers increase beyond the capacity of the range to support them. Or when they become too familiar with too many humans. Or both. Alberta's Jasper National Park is an excellent place to watch elk year around, but the park has become more popular every year and problems have developed. In May 1992, I talked to Wes Bradford, a veteran of twenty years in the park warden service in Canada's Rocky Mountain parks. Just before our interview, a cow elk was reported running down a Jasper street with a bicycle draped over her neck. She had been grazing the new green grass growing beneath one of the numerous bicycle racks in town, was startled and raised her head suddenly, and became snared. Bradford grabbed his immobilizing kit and a rifle and raced toward town. He arrived just in time to see her finally shake it loose.

Bradford showed me a list of seventy-five recent elk incidents with people; four of the people had been seriously injured. During the previous rutting season, three large bulls were identified as the worst offenders. They attacked cars (especially small ones) of people who stopped to photograph them, had punctured tires, broken windows, and caused a lot of general damage. All three bulls had to be tranquilized, live-captured, and their antlers removed. (It is interesting to note that without antlers they were no longer aggressive, although the rut was still in full swing. In fact, all were attacked and driven off by smaller bulls that the de-antlered ones had previously dominated.)

Surprisingly, some cows of Jasper have become even a greater problem than the bulls, but at a different season. During the May–June calving season, many cows become intolerant of either humans or animal predators that approach calving areas that are staked out well before the calves are born. Unfortunately one such area is in the busy Whistler Campground where unwary campers easily and inadvertently enter calf territory. People walking alone, especially if small in stature, can find themselves facing an angry elk and must be mighty nimble to evade the flying forefeet of the defensive cow.

During the 1980s in Banff National Park, which adjoins Jasper to the south, officials had similar headaches. Not only were a lot of elk roaming freely in and around Banff Townsite, often stopping play on the famous Banff golf course, but many were being killed in collisions on the busy Trans-Canada Highway that runs through the park and carries heavy traffic night and day. People as well as animals were killed in the collisions with bighorn sheep and elk crossing the road.

The highway problem was solved to some extent by erecting a ten-foot-high (3-m) chain-link fence along both sides of the Trans-Canada for its full length within park boundaries. This eliminated the vehicular collisions, but it divided an intact ecosystem in half. Another result was that the numerous clever coyotes soon learned that they could kill the sheep and elk calves by running them into the fence. The toll of both elk and sheep from this new peril proved to be greater than the earlier losses to motorized traffic.

Trouble still brews with the urban elk in Banff. What makes it so serious is that so many of the 3.5 million summer tourists, many from abroad, have little knowledge or understanding of wildlife. They do not realize that the elk are wild, powerful animals. They do not give them a sufficiently wide berth, approaching them to take photos and even trying to pet the elk. There are two possible solutions: Eliminate all of the elk from the area, or begin an expensive education campaign for all visitors. Parks Canada officials have opted for the latter course and despite being hampered by government budget cuts of the late 1990s, are doing an excellent job. For many natives and travelers alike, Banff wouldn't be the same without its elk, despite the problems.

The love-hate relationship has certainly been woven into the history of elk in Minnesota, a history that is typical of many areas in North America. When the first settler built a log cabin and hitched a horse to a plow here, elk were abundant throughout the

Both photos: The annual elk antler auction held every spring in Jackson, Wyoming, is a major civic event. Discarded antlers, which local Boy Scouts gather on the nearby National Elk Refuge, are sold at auction, and a portion of the proceeds buys winter food for the elk. (Photos by Peggy Puchi)

territory. We have no idea exactly how many elk roamed the land, but early accounts and fading photographs of hunting camps suggest that the number was high. A hundred years ago, the bugling of bulls echoed across the forests in the northern half of the state.

From southwest to northeast, Minnesota is divided by a belt of hardwood forest. West of this the land is prairie, the beginning of the Great Plains, and once the range of the Manitoban subspecies of elk. East of this divide is boreal forest and the westernmost range of the now extinct Eastern elk. In fact, the Eastern subspecies may have made its last stand here. Both races are now gone, and any elk that remain here are ancestors of Rocky Mountain stock transplanted from Yellowstone Park about 1913.

Most Minnesotans have traditionally liked the idea of elk roaming the state's wild areas. From time

to time the state legislature has appropriated money to manage them, as in Itasca State Park. At first these animals were seriously poached, but in time there were enough to be released on the (then) Red Lake Preserve. But what was at first an uneasy truce with the increasing number of farmers in the area turned into open warfare. Elk were killed on sight when they appeared near cropfields or orchards. By 1995, it was estimated that only thirty to forty wild elk survived in the entire state. But some Minnesotans have not given up hope of having a viable population of the animals in the state.

Orie and Gwendolyn Kvilhaug own land adjacent to the Grygla Wildlife Management Area not far from Thief River Falls, where a small elk herd survives with whitetails, moose, black bears, and much waterfowl. In 1990, the two nature lovers handed over the deed for eighty acres to the North Star Chapter of the Rocky Mountain Elk Foundation, which in turn deeded the land to the Minnesota Department of Natural Resources. The Kvilhaugs specified that their land be managed as wildlife habitat with elk especially in mind.

Selling Elk

Elk have long been popular with some ranchers, landowners, and just plain big-game fanciers in Canada and the United States who have the means and the space to keep and breed the species. Elk are prolific, prosper in captivity, and can be contained behind fences. Inevitably some of these collections expanded into profitable big-game farms where the elk were husbanded and treated like valuable prize cattle, or better. Considerable income was to be made from trophy bulls that could be "hunted" on the spot or sold to hunting preserves. There was a much smaller market for the meat and for elk urine, which is used by hunters as an attractor.

For a time there was also an insatiable (it seemed) market for the antlers still in the velvet; the velvet antlers were used in traditional oriental medicines. By 1987, Asian dealers were paying up to $140 per pound for antlers in the velvet, which were sawed off just as the bone reached maximum size and before the velvet would be naturally shed. For example, game rancher Henry Stip of Sydney, Montana, nor-mally sawed about 350 pounds (150 kg) a year, but spared the biggest bulls for hunting. In 1989, the price for antlers plunged to about $25 per pound, and at the same time, Asian buyers swindled many western ranchers out of huge amounts of money. The scams went like this: One year the buyer arrived in person to buy a rancher's entire antler crop and paid cash for it. The buyer then instructed the rancher to ship next year's crop directly to Korea and payment would come by return mail. Of course the check was never in the mail. One Montana game farmer was taken for about $70,000.

Other problems are also brewing. In 1991, a Montana hunter shot an elk that, unknown to him, had escaped from a game farm in the area. Genetic testing revealed it was not a pure Rocky Mountain elk and, in fact, was part red deer, which are also raised on game farms. Since then other "wild" elk of mysterious origin have proved to be elk-red deer hybrids. When these animals escape it is often not reported by game ranchers for fear of discrediting themselves and the whole industry. But genetic mixes of red deer and crossbreeds in the wild herds can be a dangerous business with serious consequences in the future, including the spread of alien disease and a decline in quality of trophy antlers.

The Rocky Mountain Elk Foundation

One cool evening in May 1984, Bob Munson and three friends sat in his kitchen in Troy, Montana, drinking coffee and discussing mutual interests. A favorite topic was elk, as Dan Bull, Bob's brother Bill Munson, and Charlie Decker all were avid elk hunters. Before they broke up well after midnight, all agreed that somebody should found a national conservation club or organization dedicated to elk. "Why not the four of us?" one of them said. It seems almost a miracle that from their small talk—daydreaming, really—grew the Rocky Mountain Elk Foundation (RMEF), which in 1995 claimed 88,000 active members in 360 chapters, plus many corporate sponsors across the United States and Canada.

Every wild creature should have such an association working in its behalf. Consider that in just ten years the RMEF has generated more than $30 million, which has been spent to buy and enhance criti-

Both photos: Elk antlers have been used by craftsmen past and present to make a great variety of tools, weapons, and decorations. The bison carved on the elk antler coronet and the fighting elk etched on a knife handle are the work of Glenn Smith of Billings, Montana.

cal wildlife habitat as well as to fund critically important wildlife research and conservation education programs. The habitat acquired by the RMEF in British Columbia and sixteen American states was on the brink of degradation or of being lost entirely. Specific projects of the RMEF have included everything from prescribed burning to building water catchments in dry areas, from removing to repairing miles of fencing where needed, and transplanting animals into environments with adequate habitat but few or no elk. It is hard to measure the impact these works have had, but we have thriving elk herds today where they might not otherwise exist.

Among the most significant contributions of RMEF was the acquisition, by outright purchase from private landowners, of 8,700 acres of critical winter range for that same North Yellowstone herd that annually migrates northward out of the national park past Gardiner, Montana. However, it is possible that the group's education campaign aimed at children will have just as long lasting an effect. Easy-to-understand publications are regularly sent to schools and classrooms. RMEF even maintains a free hotline for teachers anywhere who need any kind of help in teaching conservation. It is difficult to overestimate the valuable work of the RMEF. A lot still remains to be accomplished, some of it in game-law enforcement.

The success of this now international organization is the result of good leadership and a most enthusiastic membership of outdoor enthusiasts. Bob Munson is the executive director, and most members happen to be hunters. Peggy and I have attended annual chapter meetings, and invariably they are rich and happy experiences with entire families participating. There are slide shows, wildlife art auctions, and music. We return home from these meetings always feeling enriched.

*At Trail Town near Cody, Wyoming, antlers are piled high as they were long ago on edges of lonely frontier settlements. Later some of these would be shipped away, ground up, and used as fertilizer. **Overleaf:** A bull elk crosses the Miette River near our camp at Whistler Campground in Jasper National Park, a fine base for wildlife photography.*

Elk Poachers

Peggy and I are among the numerous people that often saw and occasionally photographed a magnificent bull elk, usually in the Elk Park area of Yellowstone between Madison Junction and Norris Geyser Basin. It was the kind of strong, healthy animal that is important to the elk gene pool. It carried fifteen total antler points, and park biologists estimated that it may have been six and one-half or seven and one-half years old. Some called this bull "Charger" because on a number of occasions it bluff-charged people who it deemed came too near.

On the evening of September 18, 1993, we were camped in the Norris Campground along with many others who had come to watch the annual rutting activities. At about 10:30 P.M., I thought I heard a rifle shot, but dismissed it as a car backfiring. I was wrong. The next morning another cameraman found the nearly intact carcass of the famous bull about two hundred yards (180 m) from the road. Only the great antlers and connecting skull cap had been removed. Investigating rangers found empty rifle casings nearby; other than that, they had no clues or leads to the killer or killers.

Of course it is illegal to hunt within a national park, or even carry a loaded weapon. Under federal law, poachers can be fined up to $250,000, serve prison time, and have all equipment used in the commission of the crime (including the vehicle) confiscated. But even when poachers have been caught, punishment is often light.

There seemed to be little chance that the poachers of Charger would ever be caught. However, photographs of the animal were published in magazines, taken from so many different angles that its antlers would be easily identifiable if they ever appeared in a taxidermist's shop or trophy room. That is exactly what happened when Chad Beus of Salt Lake City took the rack

Too many elk everywhere are victims of poaching. Only the antlers of this one, illegally killed in Montana, were taken. Had they been trophy class, the skull would also have been removed and the rack sold.

to a Utah taxidermist for mounting. The taxidermist immediately recognized the head from a photo in *Bugle*, the official publication of the Rocky Mountain Elk Foundation. DNA tests of the antlers confirmed that they did indeed belong to Charger.

Beus, who denied shooting the popular elk, was fined $30,000 and sentenced to four months in prison by a federal judge in Cheyenne, Wyoming. His rifle was confiscated. The penalties would have been much lighter if the poacher had not paid an accomplice, Shane Chavers, $5,000 not to testify against him. So justice was, in part, served. But Charger's genes, which would have been passed on during the 1993 rutting season, are lost forever.

Conservation and the Future

Looking to the future, in view of the needs of the elk and the exacting requirements of recreation based on multiple use, the safest course is to model elk management along natural lines, not only to preserve the elk as a living animal, but also, as far as is reasonably possible, to preserve its distinctive habits as well as its habitat.
—Olaus Murie, *The Elk of North America*

As snow began to fall on a cold morning late in 1906, a group of thirty-five vigilantes gathered at the Tom Hanshaw cabin near Kelly in Jackson Hole, Wyoming. After a brief trial, vigilante leaders William Seebohm and Holiday Menor issued an ultimatum to William Binkley, Charles Purdy, and Charles Isabel who stood before them, roped hand and foot. "Be clear out of this country in twenty-four hours," one of the leaders warned the captives, "or you'll hang from a tree out there." The threesome left and were never seen in the area again.

The three culprits had been caught slaughtering hundreds of elk in this then-remote region of the West. They had left entire carcasses to rot after extracting only the canine teeth, which could be made into charms that sold for from ten to one hundred dollars in eastern cities—big money at the turn of the nineteenth century. Although this vigilante justice by outraged landowners was probably as illegal then as it would be today, it was also one of the first acts of elk conservation or management in the Rocky Mountains. Hunting for elk ivory, called "tusking," had been widespread until that morning, but the landownders' ultimatum seemed to end it in northwestern Wyoming.

Go afield in elk country in the fall, and the first animals you see may be at the base of a rainbow. Or next day, beneath a heavy snowfall.

Creating the National Elk Refuge

Jackson Hole is one of the most magnificent intermountain valleys in the world and was among the last to be settled in America. The combination of short (but exquisite) summers, long winters, and relative isolation kept this wide valley of the Snake River a secret known by few. Only about sixty-five people lived there in 1899. When a few more settlers began filtering into the area in the early 1900s, it was the winter home of as many as 25,000 elk, which were a handy source of meat. That number may be a little high, according to some researchers, but there is no question that at the turn of the century almost half of all elk left in North America were in the Yellowstone ecosystem, which includes Jackson Hole. We can only try to visualize the extraordinary spectacle of so many large animals migrating and pausing to paw the deep snow of their old winter range.

Just as the number of homesteaders was on the increase, converting more historic elk range into livestock pastures, a series of extremely severe winters struck Jackson Hole. From 1909–1911, deep snows and sub-zero temperatures that lasted for weeks may have cut the elk population in half. Thousands starved and many more were shot when they raided ranchers' haystacks. A rancher's wife wrote to relatives back in Ohio that if the elk skeletons piled up all around her yard were dollars, she would be rich forever.

For thousands of years elk migrated through Jackson Hole—southward every fall, northward each spring. Elk scattered on summer ranges in what is now Grand Teton National Park, Bridger Teton National Forest, Teton Wilderness, Gros Ventre Mountains, and as far away as southern Yellowstone Park. Elk begin the gradual trek southward every October, funneling into the Snake River Valley and through western Wyoming. In time, not only the numerous livestock ranches but the growing town of Jackson stood directly in the path of the migration. Unless something could be done to solve this impasse, the elk herds of northwestern Wyoming would eventually be lost, or at least reduced to token numbers.

Wyoming State Game Warden D. C. Nowlin, in 1909, was probably the first person to call for an elk refuge on critical winter range just north of the town of Jackson. In 1911, the Wyoming legislature asked the U.S. Congress for help. Fortunately, Congress was, even then, far more sensitive to conservation issues than Congresses have been in the 1990s. Within two months, $20,000 was appropriated for an investigation of the elk situation, as well as for feeding and protecting them. A further appropriation of $45,000 was made by the federal government to acquire land, and along with money from the state, the National Elk Refuge became a reality on August 10, 1912. Additional lands were added by Presidential Executive Orders in 1935 and 1936. Today, the National Elk Refuge, a unit of our National Wildlife Refuge system, contains 25,000 acres, or almost the entire remaining winter elk range in Jackson Hole. All of the refuges in our National Wildlife Refuge system are of inestimable value to native wildlife and to all Americans, but few were ever set aside at such a critical time to save so much of our heritage.

About 7,000 elk now spend winters on the National Elk Refuge; another 1,000–2,000 winter on smaller satellite refuges in the vicinity that are managed by the Wyoming Game & Fish Department. This number is controlled by the amount of legal hunting allowed in surrounding country. Elk assemble and remain on the refuge for about six months, from November until May, and range freely there for about half that time. From late January until mid-April they receive supplemental feed, and that is what makes the refuge succeed. This feeding holds the hungry animals within refuge boundaries and keeps them from wandering out along old migration routes where they are neither welcome nor safe.

In the beginning, baled hay was the supplemental food. In 1975, the change was made from baled hay to alfalfa hay pellets, which are rationed at about seven to eight pounds (3–3½ kg) of pellets per animal per day, or about thirty tons (27 metric tons) daily for the entire herd. National Elk Refuge personnel do all the feeding using government equipment, and the federal government pays for about half of the pellets. The Wyoming Game & Fish Department also pays for about half of the feed with hunting-license money. Local Boy Scouts also contribute money from the sale of elk antlers, which they collect on the refuge every spring.

The actual supplemental feeding is a scientifically managed program, rather than a haphazard hand-

When the number of elk living on any range exceeds the carrying capacity of the range, habitat destruction occurs. Here a quaking aspen forest has been badly degraded in Yellowstone by too many elk. **Overleaf:** *Each winter many thousands of elk spend the season on the National Elk Refuge in northwestern Wyoming, where they are fed, and where they are easily seen by visitors via horse-drawn sled.*

out. More pellets are apportioned for a longer time during the most severe weather periods or when available natural forage is used up.

Perhaps almost as important as the feeding is intensive irrigation of refuge bottomland in summer and prescribed burning to increase the growth of hardy, nutritious grasses. Old hay fields on the refuge have been renovated, and grasses that elk prefer have been planted.

Sad to say, not all government agencies have always acted in the best interests of our precious wildlife. Within adjacent Bridger-Teton National Forest and nearby Targhee National Forest in Idaho, excessive timber harvesting, ever more logging roads, and livestock overgrazing continue to gradually degrade both areas. But the Jackson Hole elk were lucky again when in 1958 the Jackson Hole Cooperative Elk Studies Group was formed. It is still active and to date has been mostly free of political pressures. The

group is composed of biologists of the Wyoming Game & Fish Department, U.S. Forest Service, National Park Service, and U.S. Fish & Wildlife Service. The goal of the group has been to coordinate planning, programs, and elk research in order to exchange ideas and information on how best to manage the herd now and into the future. All four of these agencies have legal responsibilities for managing some part of Jackson Hole's elk and elk habitat.

There are valuable dividends from this kind of long-term management. Peggy and I have visited the Elk Refuge often and know it is a great sanctuary not only for elk, but for wildlife in general, including two once-endangered species, bald eagles and peregrine falcons. Greater sandhill cranes nest on marshes of the refuge and gather here in autumn before beginning the southward migration. We have accompanied Steve and Kathy Minta during their important studies of badgers, and at the same

time counted Canada geese, long-billed curlews, northern goshawks, kestrels, and the uncommon merlin. Native cutthroat trout spawn and thrive in the Snake River and its refuge tributaries.

There is another aspect about the National Elk Refuge well worth mentioning. Whereas other refuges and their programs are often held in suspicion by residents and landholders living nearby, this one is held in highest regard by the entire Jackson Hole community. One reason, of course, is that the healthy elk herd means money. Sportsmen and -women account for much of it. People also come from around the world to see the spectacle of the massed herds in winter. Each day throughout the winter, horse-drawn sleighs carry visitors among the habituated animals along Flat Creek. It is a rich, exciting experience, even in this scenic area where the skiing ranks with the best on earth.

Even as winter has dissolved into spring and all the elk march out toward their summer ranges far away, interest in the elk remains high. Throughout April, hundreds of members of the local Boy Scout troops fan out on foot across the refuge to collect the antlers that have been cast by the departing bulls—it is almost like discarding excess baggage. The huge piles of antlers are then exhibited in Jackson's town square, near an old arch built of elk antlers, and the accumulated mass of pure bone is sold at auction. Some of the bidders are craftspeople, while others are simply antler collectors. Many from Taiwan, Seoul, and Hong Kong purchase the antlers for pharmaceuticals. The entire auction weekend has a happy country fair atmosphere with a pancake breakfast served *al fresco*, western music playing in the background, and a warm spring sun shining. All this helps the local merchants and innkeepers realize the great importance of this second-largest species of native deer. The antler sales revenue finances both Boy Scout activities and feed for next winter's hungry elk.

If all of the above sounds over-congratulatory, it really isn't. If there were more conservation efforts as valuable as the National Elk Refuge in North America, the future of this and all other creatures that share the elk's range would be rosier.

Modern Elk Management Strategies

Much of modern elk management has become quite uncomplicated, maybe even too simple. Fish and game departments in the various elk states and provinces determine how many elk the winter ranges in their areas can support. Biologists are able to do a much better job of this than in years past through more accurate census methods and by being better able to evaluate and classify winter range.

After the maximum number of elk that winter range can support is determined, elk populations are reduced to this number by regulating the kill, or harvest, during the next hunting season. Generally, the longer the season, the greater the kill, although weather and economic factors can play a part. The population of elk, as well as the number of trophy bulls in a herd, can also be regulated by encouraging the harvest of cows or by limiting the fall hunt to males only. In certain areas of some states, hunting is only permitted for cows and for bulls with at least ten total antler points; smaller bulls may not be taken. The object here is to assure a good number of large trophy bulls every season.

There are some serious drawbacks as well as advantages to be considered with the winter feeding grounds method of elk management. Under completely natural conditions, elk seek shelter under trees during winter, mostly on south- and west-facing slopes, to avoid excessive loss of body heat. But most feeding grounds are "open" and do not offer such thermal protection, so elk use other means to try to maintain warmth. One of these is to bunch together in large groups with the strongest continually merging toward the center for maximum protection. At the same time weaker animals are squeezed outward toward the edges of the herd. This constant seething uses up much, perhaps too much, energy. Some biologists now believe that while food is certainly critical during periods of deep snow and intense cold, conserving energy and maintaining body temperature are just as important.

Research biologist Dan Toweill of the Idaho Department of Fish & Game adds another viewpoint to the feeding-ground theory. He believes that providing the best winter range and feeding in the world won't help a bit if the summer range is denuded of trees and crisscrossed with roads. In other words, wise elk management should include cutting back on the intensive and terrible timber cutting and livestock grazing that continues on national forest lands

Especially in winter, predators take a certain toll of elk. But wolves (shown here) and cougars have evolved together with the elk over the centuries. Prey and predators are interdependent.

Above: Biologists are able to monitor elk movements and lifestyles by affixing radio collars around the animals' necks. The information gathered is necessary for the best game and range management. Right: Elk sightings such as this one depend on conservation of elk range or habitat wherever it exists. That means reduced timber cutting and overgrazing by livestock.

today, with scant concern for the elk herds and other wildlife.

Another unhappy result of the unnatural crowding on elk feeding grounds is the possible spread of brucellosis, also knows as Bangs Disease or ungulate fever. In completely wild populations (which do not depend on feeding grounds), this disease is rare, but on feeding grounds some animals may be infected. Afflicted cows have spontaneous abortions of calves. Tom Toman of Wyoming's Game & Fish Department points out that only 33 percent of cows that winter on feeding grounds have calves in June. But the ratio increases to 45 percent for cows that do not overwinter on crowded feeding grounds.

Game managers have shot feed-ground elk with wax "bio bullets" containing brucellosis vaccine that enters the target's bloodstream. It works, but it is an expensive option. In 1994, Wyoming spent $1.4 million on its winter feeding operations, which does not leave much for magic bullets.

Few wildlife management plans ever work out perfectly because it is not an exact science. Despite the most carefully researched calculations of game managers, elk populations still can fluctuate wildly, especially following periods of drought or extremely heavy snowfalls. Or for no apparent reason at all. For the most part, however, state big-game biologists are doing as well as they can at a complex task too easy to criticize.

Wise game management of elk (as well as of other big-game species) certainly becomes more difficult all the time. More North Americans want to hunt elk every year, and the immense pressure to shoot a trophy bull is almost unreal. A lot of this can be blamed on the prose of outdoor writers, including this one. At the same time as there is increasing demand for elk, timber-cutting practices on federal lands have made hunting access easier by building more logging roads ever deeper into elk country. The situation is especially serious in important elk states such as Oregon where in many areas a hunter is hardly ever out of sight of logging roads and where the crush of hunters on opening day can resemble a mob scene. State game managers have responded by closing or trying to close many of these back-country roads, but to do this they must deal both with the U.S. Forest Service and with hunters who resent the closures. Even so, closed gates are no barrier to today's ATVs and mountain bikes.

A bewildering amount of new space-age equipment has also changed elk hunting—and not always for the better. Camouflage clothing, scents, sensors, game calls, calling tapes, and how-to-hunt videos have suddenly made "experts" out of hunters who would otherwise need to spend many years in the mountains to earn a trophy bull. Now almost everywhere the average age of male elk killed is lower; in the long run this can have serious consequences. In vast areas of what was formerly the finest elk range, bulls rarely reach more than three and one-half or four and one-half years old. Therefore younger bulls are doing the breeding, later each season, and the ages-old harem system (where old bulls do the breeding) seems to be fading away. The result is fewer calves conceived, and then born later than is normal with a poorer chance of survival.

Besides making it more difficult to reach the deep back country through road closures, game managers have tried to encourage the use of "primitive weapons" by giving archers and muzzleloader hunters longer and earlier seasons. But this also has backfired. Today's carbon-fiber compound hunting bow with all its accessories is far from the longbows and recurved bows in use not long ago. Also, new and better rifles with scopes that let you see in the dark are nothing like the firearms our fathers used. It might seem at first that these more-efficient weapons would reduce the annual crippling of elk, but studies have revealed exactly the opposite. Today's hunters tend to take more chances, such as attempting shots at longer range, than they would have with older gear. All of these are issues that citizens interested in elk and elk welfare must soon address.

The Elk's Future

State and local governments are realizing that elk are not only an immense source of revenue from hunters and hunting, but that visible elk herds also draw tourists who are not hunters. In other words, sound management is also sound economics. The best example of this is the Jackson Hole elk herd in winter. Or the elk rutting season every September in Yellowstone and Jasper National Parks. Another great elk "show" is on the Hardware Ranch, an important wintering area at the head of Blacksmith Fork Canyon near Hyrum, northern Utah. Not long after the elk herds arrive in October and November at the Hardware from surrounding high plateaus, and until they disappear in March, thousands of Utahans and winter ski tourists catch the daily elk-viewing sleigh rides. The activity has become so popular that there are waiting lists and night-time excursions. Sledding out among hundreds of elk on a clear, cold, moonlit night is a wonderful and eerie experience.

Recently a survey was made of winter tourists to the Canadian Rocky Mountain national parks. Most, but only by a narrow margin, came for the winter sports and recreation. But almost as many were attracted by the wildlife-watching opportunities in scenic, snowy settings. Of all the wildlife here, the elk are most widely and easily seen, and so must be credited with supporting a multi-million-dollar industry.

Strange as it may seem late in the twentieth century, elk are sometimes slaughtered for the meat as they were a century ago. One such occasion that received nationwide publicity in 1979 occurred on the Crow Indian Reservation in Montana. The residents of most reservations are not subject to state or federal game laws, or in fact even to tribal regulations. During the Crow Reservation "hunt," as many as two hundred elk were driven, roundup-style, with four-wheel-drive vehicles, from the Kern Big Game Winter Range across the state line in Wyoming, toward impassable snowdrifts and a firing line of Native American gunners in Montana. Game Warden Bob Peterson reported that the killers took only the hind quarters and backstraps, leaving the rest to the coyotes and ravens. Maybe part of the meat was distributed on the reservation where for some time wild game had been almost eliminated, but at least some of the venison was sold by a non-Indian middleman in Billings, Montana, the hindquarters going for about fifty dollars each. Market hunting still goes on.

So does the expansion of suburbia into what has been elk country for thousands of years. In the Rocky Mountain foothills of Jefferson County, Colorado, not far from the smog that today hangs over Denver, game wardens are faced with an epidemic of packs of free-running dogs that hunt elk. Cows especially are driven into fences, entangled, and torn apart by man's best friends. Twice in 1994, the packs of family pets turned on men who tried to stop the killing, and had to be shot in self defense. The truth is that the loss of habitat, of critical natural winter range now being surveyed for subdivisions, is far more serious in the long run than the packs of dogs. The dogs are simply symptoms that call attention to a more serious problem.

As I write this in mid-1995, another serious threat hangs over elk range and an irreplaceable wilderness just three miles (4.8 km) northeast of Yellowstone Park. It is the proposed New World Mine of the international Noranda Company, which would extract an estimated eight million tons (7.2 million metric tons) of ore from a mountain and excavate a seventy-seven-acre lake ten stories deep to be filled with toxic waste, just to obtain a possible $8 million worth of gold. The mining company promises to seal off the toxins forever, like a huge zippered pocket of poison. Few people believe in "forever." If this terrible program is implemented, as it might well be under the Mining Act of 1872, which the U.S. Congress should have voided long ago, the permanent damage will not only be to the elk of the area, but to the environment of America. The Yellowstone ecosystem is worth more than all the gold on earth.

During the 1970s, Yellowstone Park's superintendent, Jack Anderson, made a number of tragic decisions that still affect and degrade the park. One decision allowed snowmobiling on park roads for the first time. In the beginning this was only a minor intrusion into the peace and quiet that lay as silent as the snow over the park during the winter months. But it soon turned into a monster. Today, from Christmas until March the road from West Yellowstone comes under the steady, angry roar and blue exhaust fumes of hundreds of machines. Not only the elk have been shattered by it. Only a few animals are visible today in the Madison Valley where once cross-country skiers would meet many elk, quietly spending the winter. The park officials must act immediately to curb the snowmobile activity for the sake of the wildlife and for the less-intrusive human winter visitors. The gray-blue pall of snowmobile exhaust fumes that hangs in the air at Old Faithful is not only ugly, it's unhealthy.

Above: A bull elk browses on a strip of green grass not burned by the forest fire that devastated the background, in Yellowstone National Park. A year later heavy re-growth (**Facing page**) *appeared to reclaim many burned areas.* **Overleaf:** *A pall of smoke hangs low over Yellowstone's Gibbon Valley. Most natural fires have no long-term ill effects on elk populations.*

Epilogue

We looked upon animals like the wolf, buffalo, elk, and grizzly bear as elders because they were already here in the creation when our people came along. Ours is the task to respect the elders and to respect what the elders teach us.
—Jack Gladstone, Blackfeet Tribal Council, at a 1992 U. S. Fish
and Wildlife Service hearing on reintroducing wolves into Yellowstone

I worry greatly about the future of our elk. It is not that I fear that all elk will suddenly be gone tomorrow or next year, or even ten or twenty years from now. But there is handwriting on the wall. The bottom line is that unless we are willing to change our consumer ways, to stop using up our natural wealth, and polluting our rivers and the air by drawing a line against expanding our civilization out farther and farther onto our remaining wild lands, we will lose a lot more than just our elk. We will lose the hummingbirds and gophers, the fields of lupine and air we can safely breathe, the frogs, the bears, and the trout. We will also fritter away a quality of life that we should cling to by every possible means.

One of the great, grave, immediate dangers is from the officials we seem so programmed to elect to high office. It is a rare—perhaps even endangered—senator, congressperson, prime minister, or president nowadays who ever considers the long term best interests of the North American environment ahead of reelection. That means they listen to lobbyists of industries and false or greedy causes with more money to spend, rather than legislating for the long-term future of all citizens.

Without the elk, the North American outdoors simply would not be the same wonderland in which to escape. Without great herds of elk, in fact, and all the land and other creatures that share it.

The future of the elk: A ten-day-old calf searches for food and safety.

Trophy Hunting
with a Camera

There are two ways to go hunting for trophy elk with a camera. The first is to photograph elk where they are used to humans. The second is to go farther afield into the back country where they are not. One way is much more challenging than the other, but let's consider the easier one first.

In a number of national parks and other sanctuaries in the United States and Canada, elk have become habituated in varying degrees to humans and their activities. I have already pointed out that in such parks as Yellowstone, Banff, and Jasper, they have no fear whatever of people and in fact some elk should be given a wide berth. In still other parks the elk are accustomed to humans, but prefer to keep a fair distance away. In this category I would include Grand Teton National Park, Wyoming; Rocky Mountain National Park, Colorado; Olympic National Park (for Roosevelt elk), Washington; Redwood National Park (Roosevelt elk), California; National Bison Range, Montana; National Elk Refuge (only in winter), Wyoming; Riding Mountain National Park, Manitoba; and Prince Albert National Park, Saskatchewan. Any time spent shooting in these places is well spent. Most of our pictures were taken in these federal refuges.

The second way to pursue elk with a camera is to go afield exactly as gun hunters do, into areas of the national forests and other lands where there are annual open hunting seasons. This is a lot tougher, to say the least, because the elk are extremely wary and sometimes seemingly invisible despite their large size. They tend to avoid rather than tolerate the appearance of people in their domain. Any pictures of elk obtained in territory open to hunting are photo trophies indeed.

Every year, elk become more important subjects to the ever-growing corps of nature photographers, here gathered in Norris Meadow, Yellowstone, to shoot a rutting bull.

To be successful means being a skilled woodsperson, or lucky, or probably both. You need to know well the habits, habitats, and reactions of the animals. You need also the will, strength, and means to get out into the back country where these wild elk remain until winter drives them out. That means making plenty of footprints by hiking or pack tripping by horse, as well as being able to carry a heavy load on your back.

Early on and very idealistic, I hiked and rode hundreds of miles in search of elk trophies, at first on black and white film, later on the first available color film. It was great sport and every trip a challenge, but most of the elk I saw were far too distant for the kind of camera equipment I then owned and could afford. What I did learn was that elk were—and are—elusive creatures when not given protection. The few bulls I saw would have been fairly easy targets with my rifle, but looked mighty small and insignificant when my negatives were developed. I keep these on file just to show how tough photographing the hard way can be.

Nowadays we do our elk hunting only with cameras in national parks, and take my word that the challenge and the excitement are still there. Only the drudgery has been eliminated. I wouldn't trade those early days of lugging my camp and heavy cameras on my back for anything. But I'm too wise, or maybe just too old, to go back to them.

Photographic Equipment

It is somewhat ironic that the high-tech equipment Peggy and I use today is many times heavier than the old gear. For example, the fast 400mm autofocus telephoto lens that Peggy uses alone weights 13.5 pounds (6 kg). She is a strong woman and needs to be, because when that lens is connected to her camera and tripod, she is lugging more than twenty-eight pounds (12.6 kg). But that 400mm lens is 8X or 8-power, which means it brings the subject a whole lot closer in the viewfinder, and closer still when used with a teleconverter.

Virtually any camera that can be carried can also be used to photograph big game. But the 35mm single lens reflex (SLR) stands virtually alone as the best for the purpose. It is the lightest, handiest, easiest to carry, and most versatile of all systems. Today's 35mm SLRs are rugged and generally dependable in

heat and intense cold. Much of the technology offered on some of the newer camera models is bewildering, but once it is mastered (at least in part), the cameras can almost think for themselves. These really are the days of point-and-shoot photography. It's the pointing that may be the most difficult.

I'll assume here that some readers may be buying a 35mm SLR for the first time, or may be replacing old equipment. The best advice is to consider only a 35mm SLR with autofocus that is part of a complete photo system. By that I mean a camera for which the manufacturer also produces a variety of interchangeable telephoto lenses, speedlights, and other accessories. To go elk hunting, you need at least a 300mm (or 6X) lens, and in time may want a longer telephoto. A good many of the images in this book were taken with my 600mm (12X).

There are a number of reasons for using the long (or long focal length) telephoto lenses. They allow photography of any wildlife while it behaves perfectly naturally. Even with national park elk habituated to people, there is an invisible and variable barrier between target and photographer that a telephoto lens can bridge. If a photographer presses closer, the animals begin to behave nervously, unnaturally, or even to gradually drift away. I have watched a lot of great opportunities lost by photographers trying to approach too near to elk and other creatures.

As more elk lose all fear of humans, long telephoto lenses also become a safety factor. One September morning in Jasper National Park, I watched a party of photographers shooting a bull elk that pranced across a meadow wet with dew. Occasionally it would pause to bugle. One of the photographers crept closer to the agitated elk on elbows and knees for a low-angle viewpoint and to compensate for his too-short telephoto lens. Maybe the elk thought the man was a coyote, maybe it felt challenged, but it turned and came directly after the man. Jumping up to run, the photographer dropped an orange rucksack that had been slung over one shoulder. The man easily made it to safety while the bull zeroed in on his rucksack, which it hooked on an antler tip and was unable to dislodge. For a while the animal carried its prize like a battle flag swinging from its rack, before finally tossing it away.

When manually operated, long telephoto lenses are fairly slow to focus, and especially when fast action is taking place, there is considerable margin for error. But the autofocus feature in most modern 35mm SLRs is quickly and accurately on target. The value of this cannot be overestimated, especially when advancing years have taken a toll on vision.

Any camera used in wildlife photography should also be equipped with auto wind that advances the film automatically after each exposure. The advantage here is that the shooter can continue to concentrate on the subject in the viewfinder and not be distracted by having to advance film manually with a thumb. Some cameras also automatically rewind the film when the last frame has been exposed. During this operation the shooter can get a new roll ready for loading.

Of equal value is a "continuous" feature whereby the camera continues to fire several frames per second as long as the shutter button is depressed. Combined with predictive or follow focus, which predicts the focus for the next frame, capturing fast, continuous action while maintaining sharp focus is possible.

Although I have long had a preference for hand-holding my camera and lens whenever possible, and do hand-hold my equipment when the lens is 300mm or shorter, the longer telephoto lenses demand a steady tripod. The steadiest tripods with easily adjustable legs that compensate for uneven ground tend to be the heaviest to carry and therefore restrict how far a photographer can wander. But the critical part of any tripod is the head, the mechanism by which the camera with its lens is solidly supported by the legs. As I write, one tripod head, the Wimberley, although heavy, is far better than all the rest. Tracking a moving subject is much easier and smoother with the Wimberley than with the various ball heads it is replacing.

Peggy and I have used, and still use, most of the professional positive or slide films on the market. What we have found, despite advertising claims to the contrary, is that no one brand is best for every situation, or even for most wildlife and nature photography. Subtle changes take place from season to season, even hour to hour, at changing elevations, humidities, and latitudes. We feel that it is impossible to select exactly the right film for any given situation, so we switch frequently and probably (many other photographers would say) unscientifically, among films usually of ASA/ISO 100 and 200 speeds.

Still it is amazing how often one film gives excellent results one morning compared to another, while in the afternoon under apparently the same conditions, the opposite may be true. Our system produces disappointments and pleasant surprises, but generally the results you see on these pages.

Use the shorter focal length lenses to shoot scenes of elk in their natural habitat. For the other extreme we carry a 1.4X and 2X tele-extender that, when locked between camera and lens, increase the focal length of our longer (300mm to 600mm) telephoto lenses. There is a penalty with their use of one to two f/stops, (so they work best with fast lenses) but they do bring distant elk in closer than is otherwise possible.

Other Equipment

Shooting elk means being in the field in rugged country and in all kinds of weather subject to sudden change. Total concentration on the subject isn't possible unless you are dry and warm and well shod. In other words what you wear can be as important as what equipment you shoot.

Proper footwear might be most important of all. Most of the year we wear the best-quality ankle-high boots designed for serious backpackers, with Vibram soles, that are also somewhat resistant to moisture. When snow begins to fall, we change to insulated, calf-high boots that are water- and snow-proof, worn with felt innersoles and woolen socks. This combination keeps our feet warm even when standing for extended periods.

The layer system of dressing is the best for our activities. That means long underwear, jeans or woolen trousers, shirts, sweaters, vests, and parkas with hoods—a combination of any or all of these added or subtracted as weather dictates. A woolen knit cap that can be pulled down over the ears is comfortable. A baseball cap is ideal on bright days. Insulated mittens fastened to parka sleeves to prevent loss, worn over light, tight-fitting, knit gloves keep our hands warm, especially with chemical handwarmers ready for the bitterest days.

If all this seems like too much clothing to always have handy, we solve it with the light traveling camper van that is our base camp wherever we park it. The van has a rear bench seat that can be pulled out to form a bed, plus storage closets, refrigerator, and small cook stove, as well as space to carry a lot of photo equipment ready to use. It is also a convenience beyond just being a cargo carrier. The ability to camp overnight near our subjects makes it much easier to catch the elk and any wildlife at daybreak and in the best of all photographic light. It also allows us to linger on late afternoons until the last rays of sunlight illuminate the elk in a golden glow.

There are many fine public campgrounds in elk country everywhere. If one of the KOA (Kampgrounds of America) system is anywhere in the vicinity, that's where we spend the night. Uniform high standards always guarantee any camper secure, clean, and attractive surroundings—and hot showers.

Some other equipment is important when trophy hunting for elk. A lightweight backpack, belt pack, or multi-pocketed photo vest are good to carry extra lenses, filters, film, insect repellent, a ground cloth, and snacks.

When shooting elk outside the boundaries of parks and sanctuaries, you will need all the stealth and patience and hunting skills you can manage, just to approach within telephoto range. Outer garments of camouflage material will probably help in your concealment. However a blaze-orange jacket is certainly the wisest choice for your own safety if you are afield during open gunning seasons. In fact the law in some states requires the use of this clothing.

When photographing in parks, Peggy and I follow a different set of rules. We never try to approach any animals unseen, by stealth, but instead make every effort to stay within their sight at all times. Bobbing in and out of their view makes the animals understandably suspicious. Let us assume here a nor-

mal situation. We are slowly driving the road in a national park and we see an elk bugling on a partially wooded slope, in typical elk country. A harem of cows browses all around. In the nearest convenient parking area or pull-off, we park our van and set up camera gear: cameras and telephoto lenses on tripods. We figure that these elk will allow us to approach to a certain distance, but no closer before all move away. We must maintain that interval so that the elk feel comfortable or we can forget about shooting any pictures.

We do not move quickly, and we never move directly toward the elk. In fact we always approach obliquely, stopping occasionally to look around and to shoot a few exposures from whatever the distance. At any sign of nervousness, such as a cow that suddenly stands up or stops feeding to stare at us, we go no farther. This strategy works 95 to 100 percent of the time—and there have even been many occasions when the elk gradually move closer to us.

During the rutting season some bulls can be "called" into much better camera range by rattling antlers together or by blowing into a section of plastic tubing to imitate the bugle of a rival male. While rattling and calling are never allowed in any of the national parks, these tactics can work well for the photographer who chooses to hunt elk the hard way.

Peggy and I always shoot fairly close together. This buddy system allows slightly different camera angles and viewpoints, some of which will make better illustrations than others later on. Not the least of the benefits is the rich companionship and the friendly competition to take the best possible image of one of the world's greatest game species.

Organizations

Boone and Crockett Club
Old Milwaukee Depot
250 Station Drive
Missoula, MT 59801
(406) 542-1888

Buffalo Bill Historical Center
P.O. Box 1000
Cody, WY 82414
(307) 587-4771

Foundation for North American Big Game
Box 2710
Woodbridge, VA 22192

Kampgrounds of America (KOA)
P.O. Box 30558
Billings, MT 59114
(406) 248-7444

North American Hunting Club
P.O. Box 3407
Minnetonka, MN 55343-2107
(800)-922-4868

Rocky Mountain Elk Foundation
2291 West Broadway
Missoula, MT 59802

Safari Club International
4800 West Gates Pass Road
Tucson, AZ 85745

References and Suggested Reading

Bauer, Erwin. *Antlers*. Stillwater, MN: Voyageur Press, 1995.

Bauer, Erwin. *Deer in Their World*. New York: Outdoor Life Books, 1980.

Bauer, Erwin. *Horned and Antlered Game*. New York: Outdoor Life Books, 1986.

Bauer, Erwin. *Wild Dogs of North America*. San Francisco: Chronicle Books, 1994.

Bauer, Erwin. *Yellowstone*. Stillwater, MN: Voyageur Press, 1993.

Boone and Crockett Club. *Records of North American Big Game*. Tenth Edition. Helena, MT: Falcon Press 1993.

Brown, Robert D., Editor. *Antler Development in Cervidae*. Kingsville, TX: Texas A&I University, 1986.

Dalrymple, Byron W. *North American Big Game Animals*. New York: Outdoor Life Books, 1978.

Gilmore, Jackie. *Wildlife Legacy: The National Elk Refuge*. Moose, WY: Backwaters Publications, n.d.

Goss, Richard. *Deer Antlers: Regeneration, Function & Evolution*. Orlando, FL: Academic Press, 1989.

Mech, L. David. *The Way of the Wolf*. Stillwater, MN: Voyageur Press, 1980.

Murie, Olaus. *The Elk of North America*. Harrisburg, PA: Stackpole Books, 1951.

Rocky Mountain Elk Foundation. *Majesty*. Helena, MT: Falcon Press, 1993.

Safari Club International. *Record Book of Trophy Animals*. Rocky Mountain House, Alberta: Greenhorn Publishing, 1982.

Whitehead, G. Kenneth. *Deer of the World*. New York: Viking Press, 1972.

Whitehead, G, Kenneth. *The Whitehead Encyclopedia of Deer*. Stillwater, MN: Voyageur Press, 1993.

Wildlife Management Institute. *Big Game of North America*. Harrisburg, PA: Stackpole Books, 1978.

Wildlife Management Institute. *Elk of North America*. Harrisburg, PA: Stackpole Books, 1982.

Index

About the Authors

Erwin and Peggy Bauer are busy, full-time photographers and writers of travel, adventure, and environmental subjects. Based in Paradise Valley, Montana, the Bauers have specialized in photographing wildlife worldwide for over forty years. Their images come from the Arctic to the Antarctic, Borneo to Brazil, Africa to India, Madagascar to Malaysia, and beyond.

Erwin and Peggy Bauer may be the most frequently published wildlife photographers in the world today. The Bauers' recent magazine credits include *Natural History, Outdoor Life, Audubon, National Geographic, Smithsonian, Wildlife Conservation, National Wild-* *life* and *International Wildlife, Sierra, Safari, Chevron USA,* and *Nature Conservancy.* Their photographs annually illustrate the calendars of Voyageur Press, the Sierra Club, the Audubon Society, World Wildlife Fund, and others. The Bauers have more than a dozen books currently in print, including *Yellowstone, Whitetails, Mule Deer,* and *Antlers: Nature's Majestic Crown,* all four published by Voyageur Press. The couple has won many awards for wildlife photography in national and international photographic competitions.